Baroque & Rococo

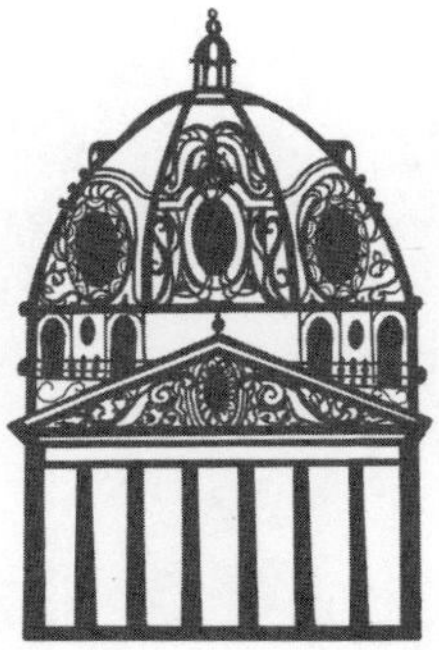

Published by
UNIVERSITY SCHOOL
at The University of Tulsa
TULSA, OKLAHOMA

ISBN Number: 1-893413-03-9

Manufactured in the United States of America

All proceeds from this series go to University School at The University of Tulsa, a non-profit educational organization.

SAILS titles include:

Classical Greece
Ancient Rome
The Renaissance
Baroque and Rococo
Neoclassicism
Romanticism

Other books are in the planning phase. Additional information is available about SAILS materials and University School.

Contact: University School at The University of Tulsa
600 South College Avenue, Tulsa, Oklahoma 74104
Phone: 918-631-5060 Fax: 918-631-5065
Visit: 326 South College Avenue, Tulsa, Oklahoma 74104
e-mail: debra-price@utulsa.edu

Acknowledgements

Many thanks to Susan Coman and her staff at Protype Inc., Tulsa, Oklahoma, who produced the series. Also thanks to copy editors Katie Abercrombie, Robyn Bowman, Ekta Gupta, Kim Harper, and Andrea Sharrer for the countless hours donated to this project.

Artwork courtesy of Photodisc, Artchives, clip art books, and Patricia Hollingsworth. Any omission of acknowledgement is unintentional.

Preface

University School teachers created SAILS for students of all ages. SAILS is based on active interdisciplinary learning in a content-rich environment as used at University School. University School at The University of Tulsa is a school for gifted children from preschool through eighth grade. The active interdisciplinary learning approach presented in SAILS enables gifted behaviors to emerge in students in both regular and special classrooms.

The purpose of SAILS is to provide a framework for understanding historical patterns which is often omitted in world, national, and art history courses. This framework is developed by showing modern day links to ancient Western civilizations, presenting reccurring patterns in history, and acquiring an understanding of the basic ideals of these cultures. Every community in America has visual reminders of ancient civilizations which go unrecognized. Students of all ages can learn to recognize and appreciate this heritage.

SAILS was created by

Editor and Illustrator - Patricia L. Hollingsworth, Ed.D.

Writers and Teachers

Katie Abercrombie
Sharon Block
Debi Foster
Cathy Freeman
Kim Harper
Marilyn Howard
Cyndie Kidwell
Gina Lewis
Alicia Parent
Marti Sudduth
Patricia Hollingsworth

Contents

ARCHITECTURE

BAROQUE MUSIC

SCIENCE AND INVENTIONS

ROCOCO ERA: 1700-1750

REVIEW

This timeline is a simplified version of time periods. The dates are all approximate and in reality overlap with one another. One country may be starting a time period just as another is ending it. The idea is to provide some guidelines for understanding ideas and influences.

	800BC-350AD Classical • Greek • Roman	350-1350AD Medieval/Middle Ages • Romanesque • Gothic	1350-1600AD Renaissance
IDEALS	• **Classical Greek Ideals:** Freedom Symmetry Balance Beauty Order Dignity "Nothing to excess"  • **Classical Roman Ideals:** Grandeur Power Efficiency Practicality 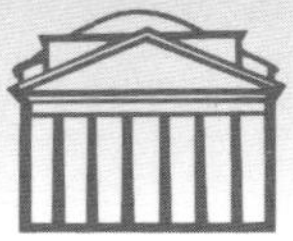	• Life is short, difficult • God all important • Afterlife all important 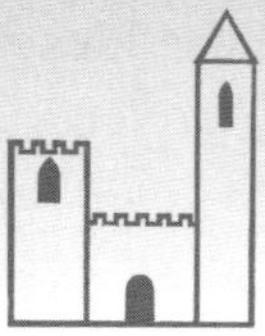	• **Classical Ideals Revived:** God and humans important Harmony Balance Beauty Order Grandeur Power 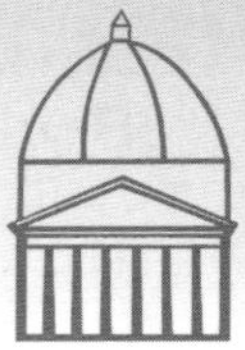
ARCHITECTURE	• **Greek Classical:** Parthenon Balance, harmony, order • **Roman Classical:** Pantheon Technology advancements	• **Romanesque:** Fortress-like • **Gothic:** God-like proportion Light, airy Spires point to God	• **Renaissance Classical:** Symmetrical Built for God and humans Human proportions Solid
ART	• **Greeks: Idealistic** Classical ideals • **Romans: Realistic** Mythological and human subjects Classical ideals 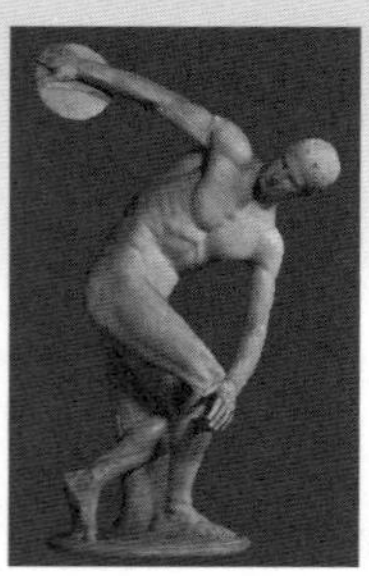	• Stiff, heavily draped sculpture • Cartoon-like drawings • Biblical subjects only 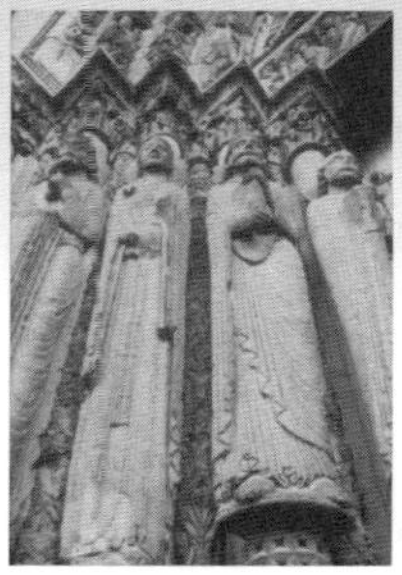	• Natural and realistic • Balanced between repose and action • Biblical, mythological, and human subjects 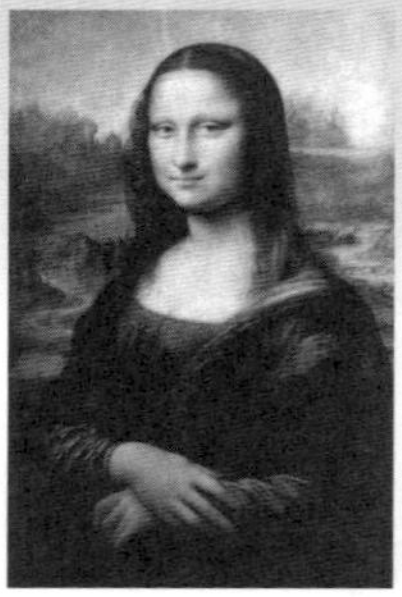

1600-1750AD	1750-1800AD	1800-1850AD
• BAROQUE • ROCOCO	NEOCLASSICAL	ROMANTIC
IDEALS		
• **Baroque** Emotion Grandeur Energy 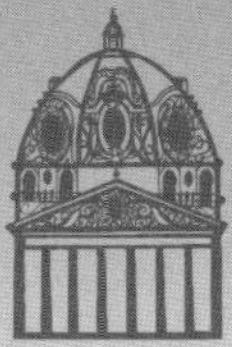 • **Rococo** Enjoyment Pleasure 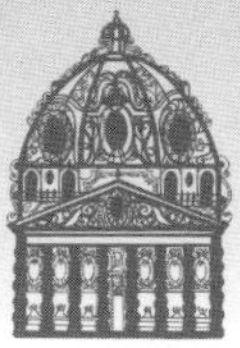	• **Classical Ideals Revived:** Freedom Dignity Balance Beauty Order 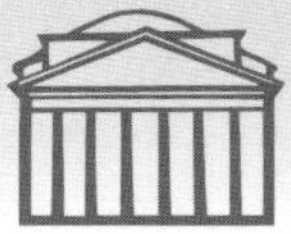	• Emotion • Imagination • Freedom • Energy • Turbulence 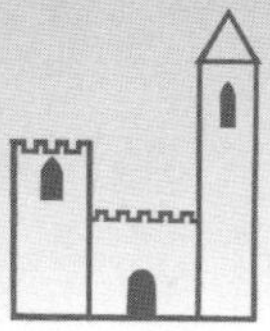
ARCHITECTURE		
• **Versailles:** Elaborate Grand • **Palaces:** Ornate Gold leaf Curlicues	• **Monticello:** Symmetry Balance Solid	• **Parliament Houses:** Gothic and Medieval
ART		
• **Baroque:** Emotional Swirling Dramatic Subject Lighting • **Rococo:** Pretty and Pleasant 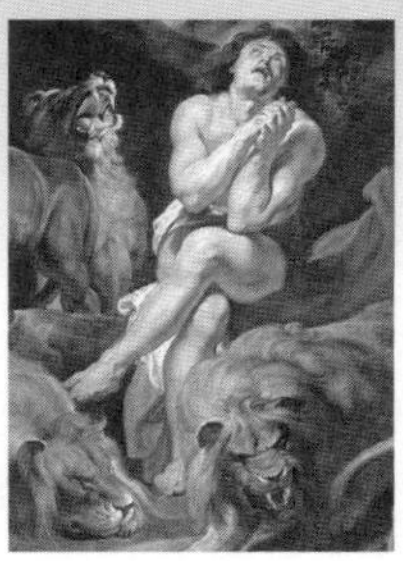	• **Classical Ideals:** Balance Harmony Dignity 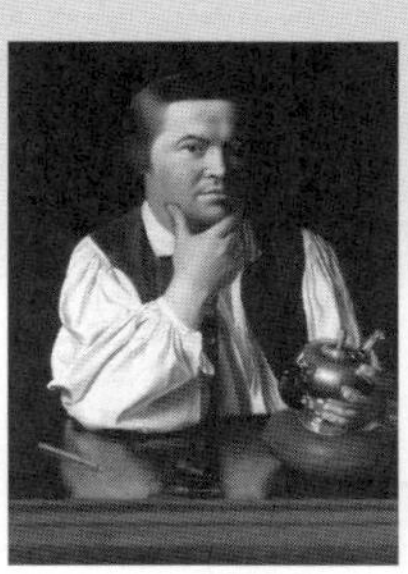	• Emotional • Swirling • Dramatic and exotic Lighting Subjects 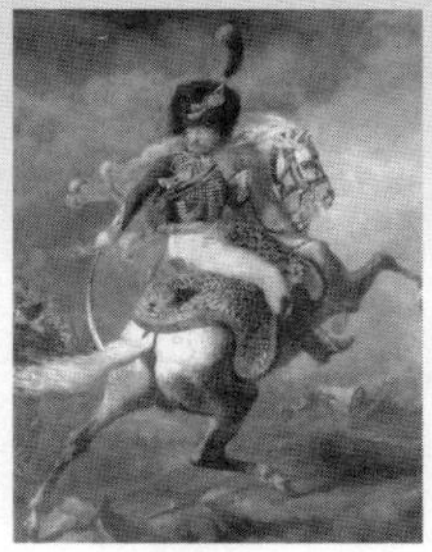

Baroque & Rococo

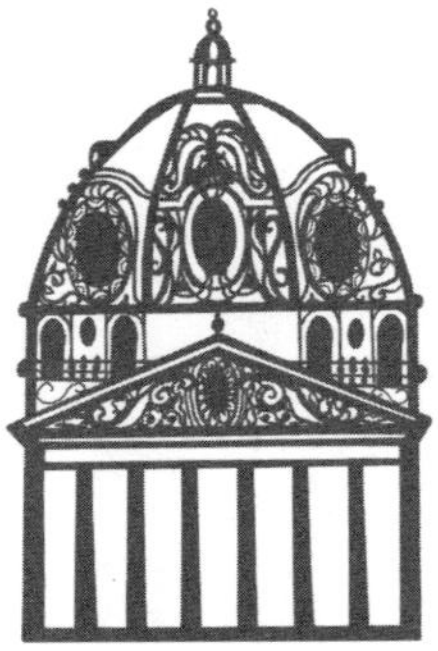

The Elaborate Baroque

INTRO

Peter Paul Rubens

My name is Peter Paul Rubens. I find the Baroque style more interesting than the Renaissance. Critics began calling this period "Baroque," which means a misshaped pearl. It was a derisive term implying that our art was not formed or shaped correctly.

Round Pearl

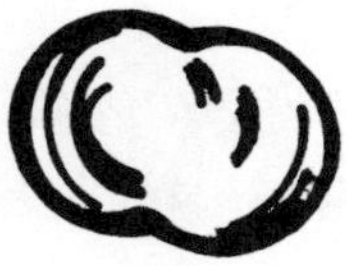

Misshaped "Baroque" Pearl

I like to paint on huge canvasses. Some of my paintings are so large that I have a special door made in my studio to get them in and out. I like to paint scenes from the Bible, mythology, and royalty. I want my art to show intense emotions, brilliant colors, grand scale, and dramatic lighting. I want art to show energy,

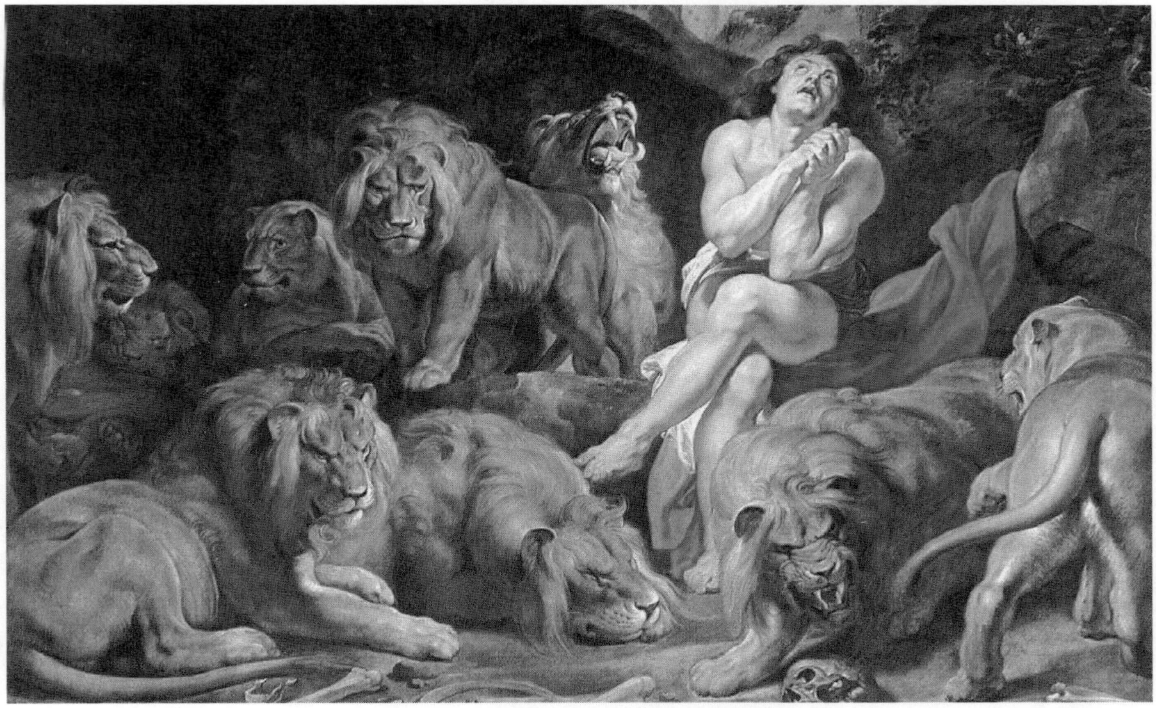

Ruben's Daniel in the Lion's Den

power, and majesty. When you look at my art, I want you to respond emotionally, not just intellectually. Well, if that is misshaped, then so be it.

By the 1600s we had gotten tired of the plainness and simplicity of the Renaissance architecture. Baroque architecture is grand and dramatic. We have given simple and plain Renaissance columns a dash of dramatic movement by making them twisted, as if they are writhing in the wind.

Our ceilings are equally exciting. We often use ovals surrounded by curlicues encompassing gold-drenched clouds, saints, angels, and cherubs as they move and swirl on every available surface. The Baroque style is invigorating, exciting, and dramatic. Perhaps you know that we, the Catholics, are in a bit of a contest (that may be too mild a word) with the Protestants. As we become more and more elaborate and complex in our churches, the Protestant's churches become more simple, more austere. Well, they are sailing off to America anyway. To each his own, I suppose.

I am going to ask Rembrandt, another famous artist, to visit with you later. His work is spectacular but he has fallen out of favor with the patrons. No one is buying his art work now. His wife has recently died. Life is hard for him now. It will do him good to talk with you.

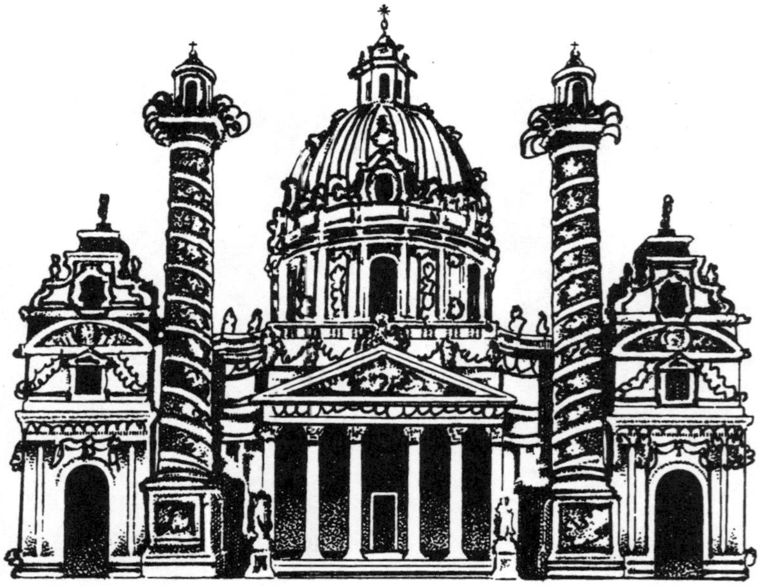

Baroque Architecture

BAROQUE QUESTIONS

1. What does the word Baroque mean and why was it used?

____

____

2. Name two famous Baroque artists. ____________________

____

3. What kind of art work does Rubens do?

____

____

4. What bad things happened to Rembrandt?

____

____

5. Describe the Baroque style.

____

____

6. Describe the churches of the Protestants.

____

____

7. Draw a picture of the outside of your house as if it had suddenly been decorated in the Baroque style.

*B*AROQUE

QUICK **FACTS**

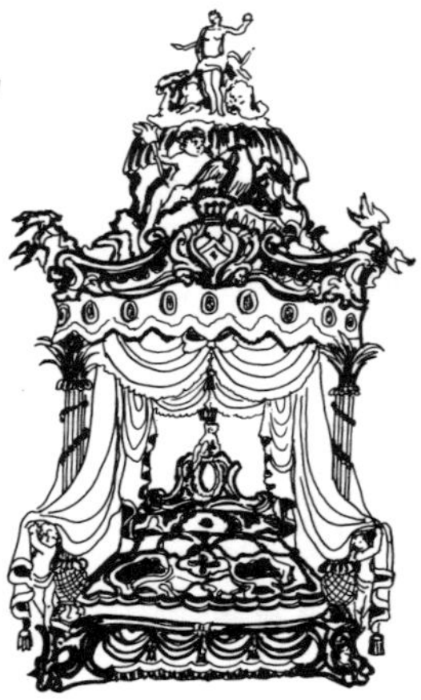

King Louis' bed

DATES

1600-1700

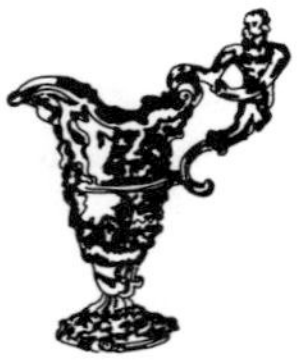

VALUES

emotion, grandeur, abundance, ornamentation, swirling movement, dramatic gestures, theatrical, passionate

GOVERNMENT

Absolute Monarchies

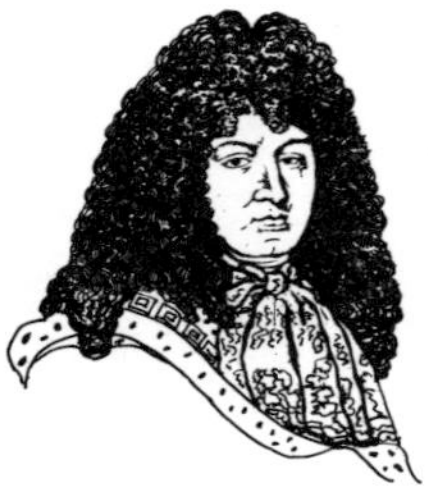

King Louis XIV of France

ARTISTS

1541-1614 — El Greco, Spanish painter; Renaissance and Baroque transitional artists

1571-1610 — Caravaggio, Italian painter; dramatic realism; strong, harsh, unflattering lights and darks

1593-1653 — Artemisia Gentileschi, Italian female dramatic realistic artist

1598-1610 — Bernini, architect and sculptor; emotion and swirling movement

1577-1640 — Rubens, Flemish artist, painter; strong, robust, huge canvases

1580-1666 — Hals, Dutch painter; happy common people

1599-1660 — Velásquez, Spanish court painter

1606-1669 — Rembrandt, Dutch; world famous painters, *Night Watch* 1642

1632-1675 — Vermeer, small paintings, interiors

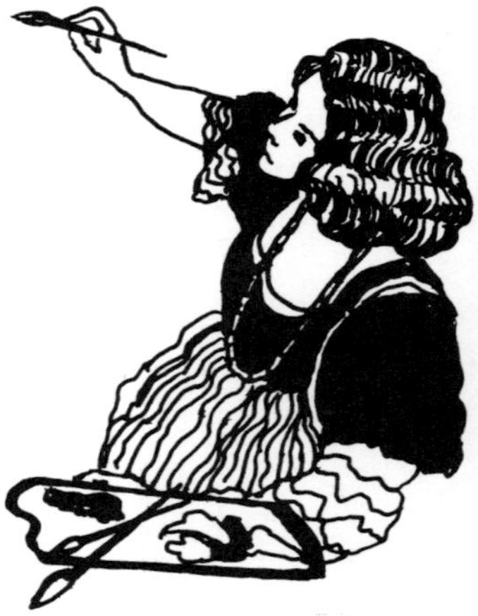

Gentileschi

SCIENTISTS

1578-1657 — William Harvey, blood circulation
1564-1642 — Galileo Galilei, thermometer

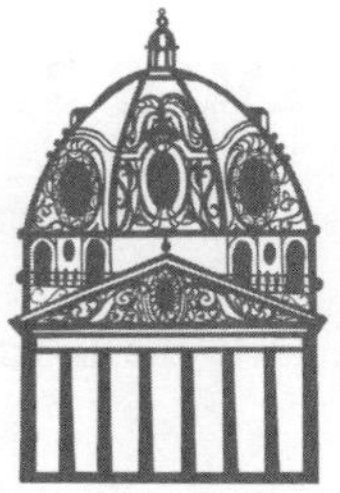
Baroque Architecture

ARCHITECTURE

Versailles — uses ornamentation of ovals,
circles, curlicues, gold leaf, marble, medallions
Christopher Wren — architect for St. Paul's Cathedral, London

INVENTIONS, DISCOVERIES, & EVENTS

1610 — Flintlock firing mechanism
1615 — English began to drink tea
1616 — Copernicus' book banned, showed that earth moves around sun
1620 — *Mayflower* sails with Pilgrims to America
1622 — William Oughtred, slide rule
1623 — Wilheim Schickard, calculator
1624 — Cornelius Drebbel, submarine
1628 — Harvey proves heart pumps blood
1637 — First oiled cloth umbrellas owned by France's King Louis XIII
1650 — Otto von Guericke, vacuum pump leads to steam engine
1656 — Christian Huygens, pendulum clock
1660 — Robert Hook, universal joint to hold telescope
1667 — First blood transfusion reported in France
1676 — Romer measured speed of light
1670 — Dom Perignon, champagne
1662 — Blaise Pascal, omnibus
1670 — Sir Samuel Morland, megaphone
1675 — Peter Henleing, portable clock (pocket watch)
1683 — Andrew von Leeuwenhoek, precision microscope
1690 — Johann Denner, clarinet
1698 — Thomas Savery, steam pump
1700 — Bartolomeo Cristofori, piano

QUICK FACTS

BAROQUE TRIVIA

1. Name one musical instrument invented during the Baroque period.

____

2. Name two events that happened during the Baroque period.

____

____

3. Name three Baroque artists.

____

____

____

4. Name four Baroque inventors and draw their inventions.

____

____

____

____

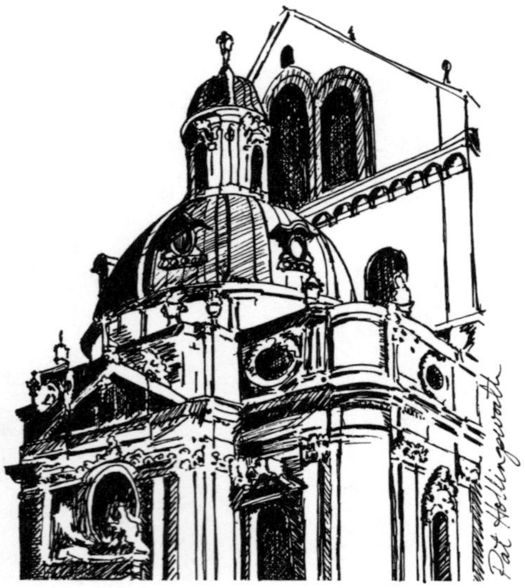

Baroque Architecture

5. Name five Baroque ideals and values.

____

____

____

____

____

BAROQUE

IDEALS

Art in the Baroque era was dramatic, bold, and grand. Artists made their work elaborate. Pictures were painted in ovals on ceilings and walls. Every available inch was filled with curlicues and ornamentation. When artists painted people and animals, they did it so that they displayed emotion and movement. Even the columns that were built had a twisting, barber-shop style so it also appeared they were moving.

Three things are shown below which are very un-Baroque in style. Using what you have already learned about Baroque, change these things to make them elaborate, emotional, and swirling.

Activity~

1. Create a Baroque frame.
2. Create an emotional face.
3. Create a twisted Baroque column.

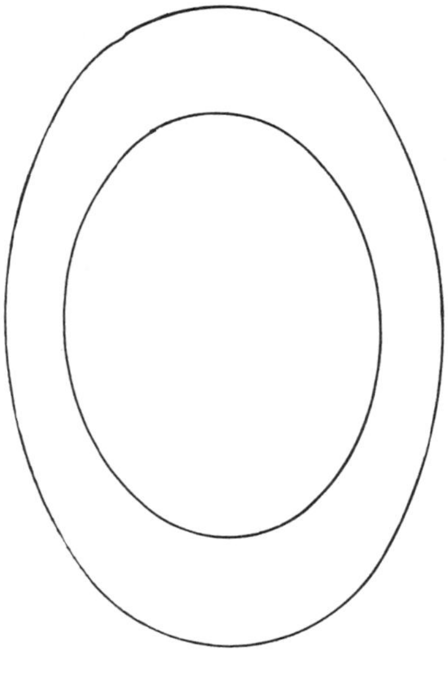

Baroque Frame

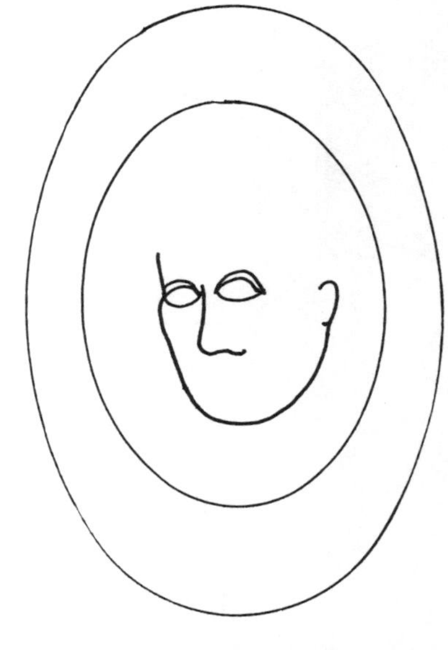

Baroque Emotional Expression

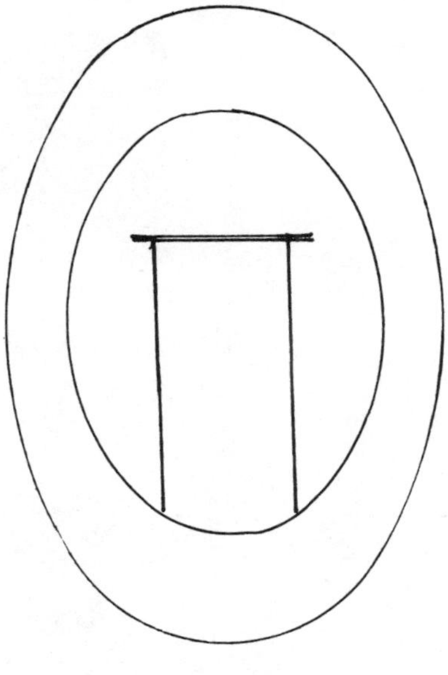

Baroque Column

BAROQUE IDEALS

Draw your own examples.

ENERGY

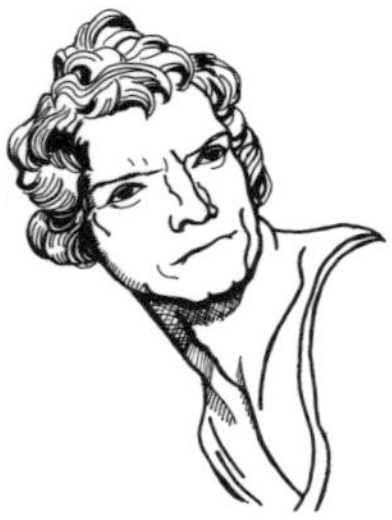

POWER

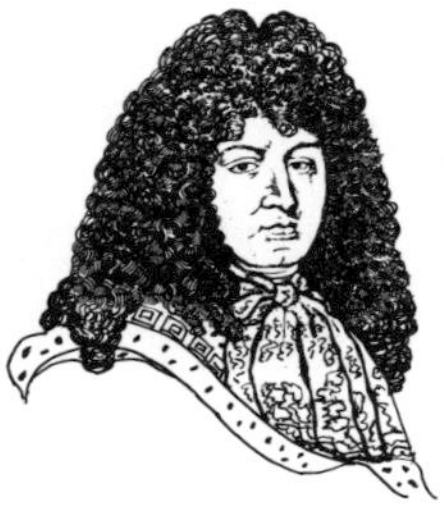

MAJESTY

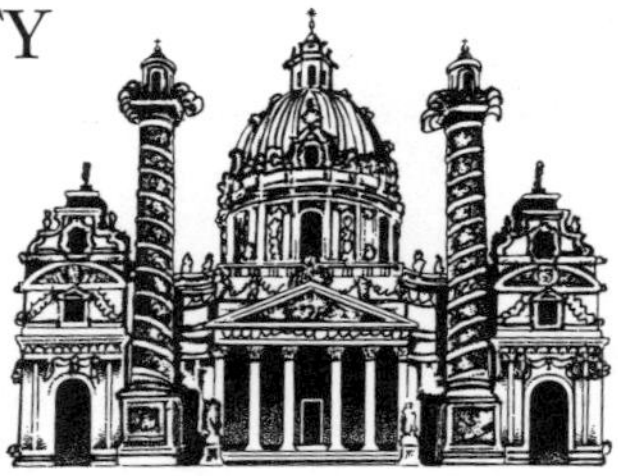

DRAMATIC SUBJECTS

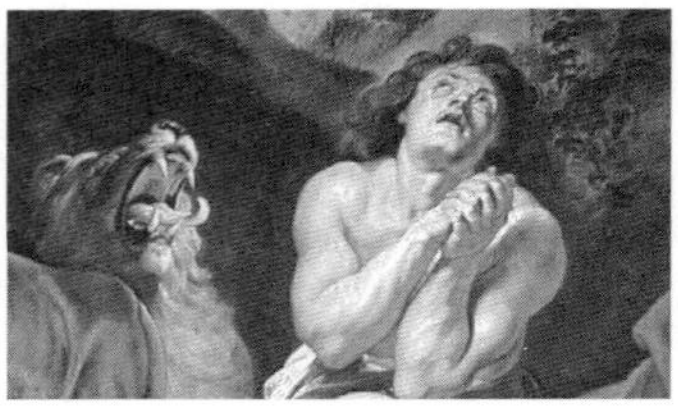

ORNAMENTATION

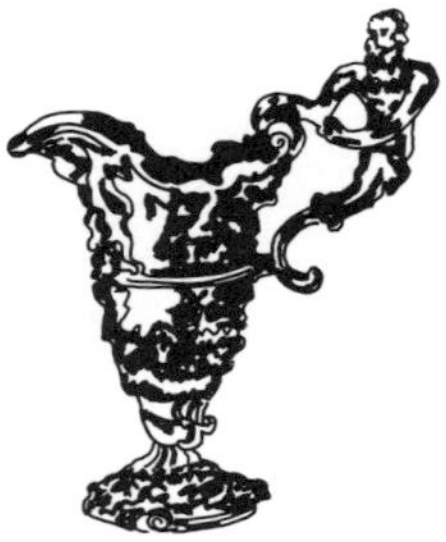

BAROQUE IDEALS

Draw your own examples.

EMOTIONAL CONTENT

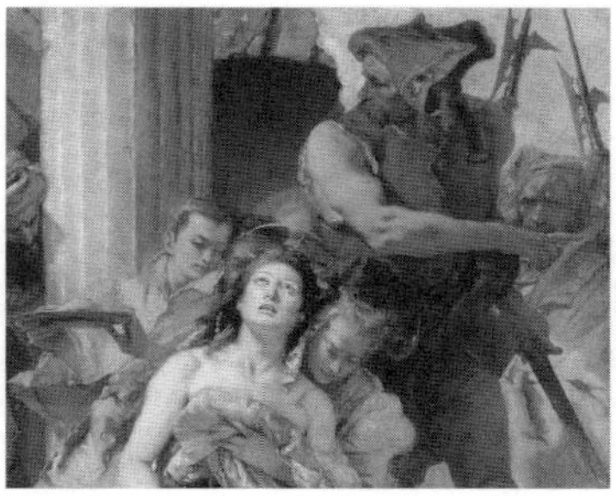

SWIRLING MOVEMENT

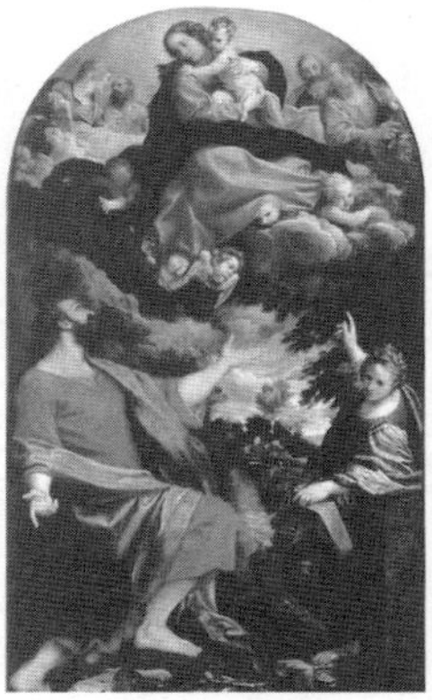

CHIAROSCURO *(key arrow SWEWR o)*
Light and shadow, from the Italian words *chiaro* (light) and *oscuro* (dark)

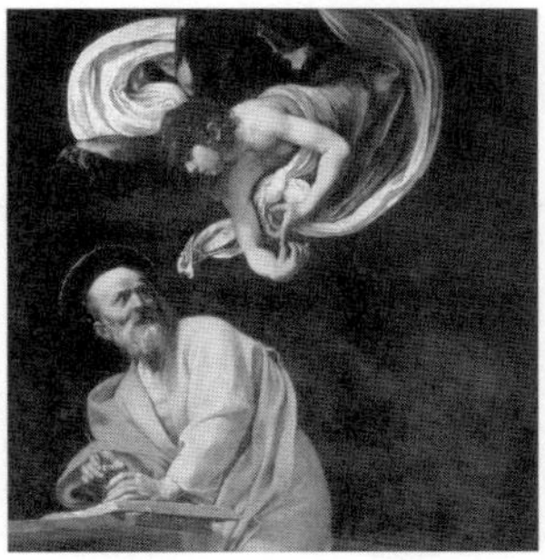

DRAMATIC LIGHTING

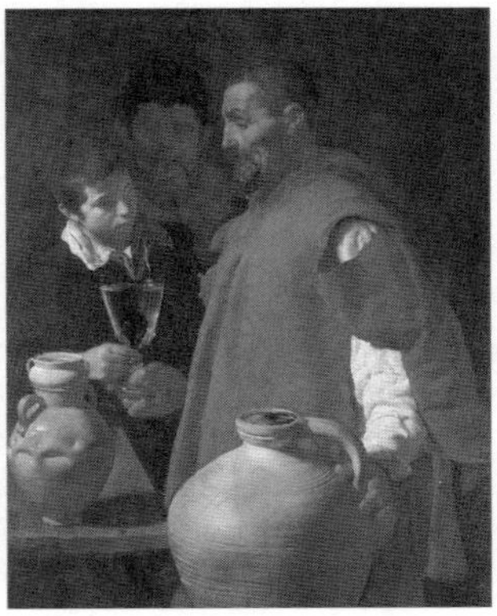

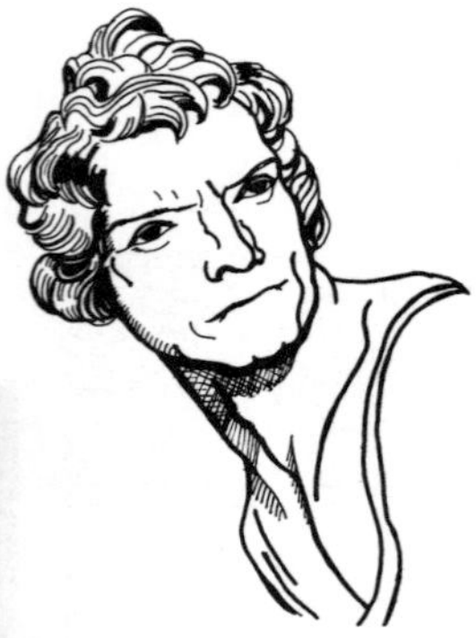

Bernini's DAVID

ITALIAN BAROQUE SCULPTURE: BERNINI

Gianlorenzo Bernini's (1593-1680) sculpture embodies Baroque ideals. His work engages your emotions with its swirling, dramatic, and energetic forms. Look at the grim determination on the face of his *David*. Look at *David* as he is captured in the moment just before he unleashes his deadly rock.

Activity~

Compare Bernini's David with those of Michelangelo's and Donatello's. Use suggested words or create your own.

	BERNINI	MICHELANGELO	DONATELLO
	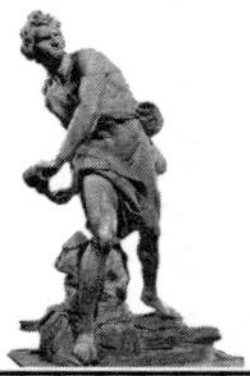	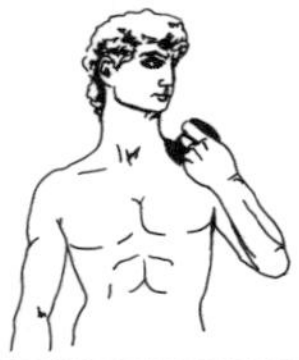	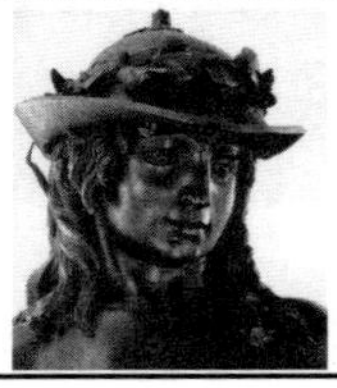
Time Period	Baroque	Renaissance	Renaissance
Body Type (boy or man)			
Body Stance (s-curve or spiral)			
Facial Expression (calm or tense)			
Attire			
Weapon			
Other			

DRAMATIC BAROQUE CHARACTERISTICS

LET'S BE MORE SPECIFIC

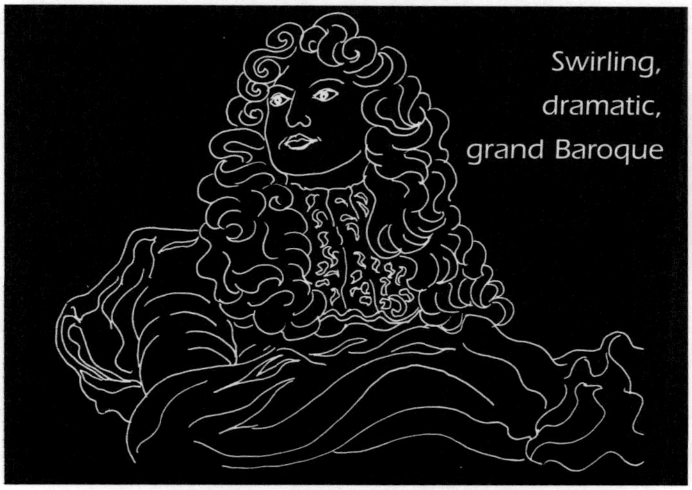

Look at the picture of the dramatic sculpture. It is characteristic of Baroque art. It is **swirling**, **dramatic**, **abundant**, and **grand**. These words all describe Baroque art. They can be hard words to write about, so let's be more specific.

Pick one of the bold words above that describe Baroque art and write it on the line below.

My topic: ______________________________

1. What animal is this topic like and why? ____________________
2. What plant is this topic like and why? ____________________
3. What shape is this topic like and why? ____________________
4. What color is this topic like and why? ____________________
5. Now pick your favorite description above — with animal, plant, shape, or color. Pick more words that complete this description.

Nouns: ______________________________

Verbs: ______________________________

Adjectives: ______________________________

6. Now use your ideas to write a short paragraph to describe characteristics of the Baroque period.

____

____

____

____

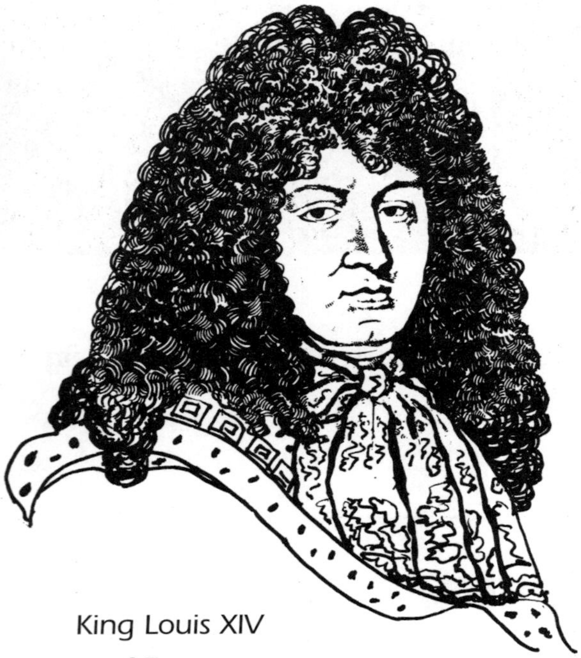

King Louis XIV
of France

Louis XIV
1643-1715

Louis XIV succeeded to the throne of France in 1643 at the age of five. Because he was only five years old he was under the regency of his mother. King Louis reigned from 1643 to 1715, longer than any other monarch. During his reign he promoted the arts, built the magnificent palace at Versailles, and made France the most powerful monarchy in Europe.

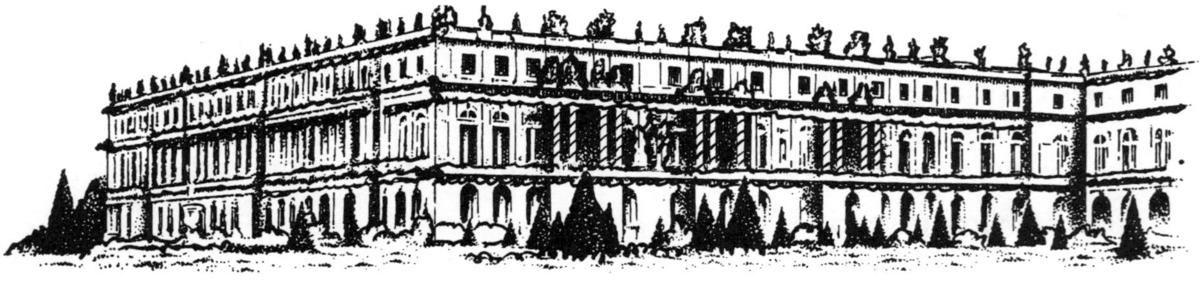

Palace of Versailles

A DAY IN THE LIFE OF LOUIS XIV (1643-1715)

Louis XIV's Morning Routine

He lived in an enormous palace in the city of Versailles. Louis was known as the Sun King and slept in an enormous bed that had an elaborate sunburst carved into the headboard. Every morning when Louis awoke several people were there to witness the royal rising. A physician and a surgeon would enter first and inquire about his majesty's health. A wood-carrier would light a fire in his room and the time-keeper would wind all the clocks. The wig maker would be adjusting the wig that the king would wear for that day. The royal barber would give the king a shave and a sponge bath in spirits of wine. The king would then dress for the day's ceremonies in silk stockings, Italian leather boots, culottes (knee-length trousers), ornamented vest, silk cravat, and a coat decorated with gold, jewels, and lace-trimmed cuffs.

This is the usual morning routine for the King of France. Does it sound at all similar to your normal morning routine? Make a list below of the routine that you usually follow in the mornings before school. Be sure to put everything in order. Describe the bed that you sleep in and the clothes that you usually choose to wear. Don't forget to use descriptive words.

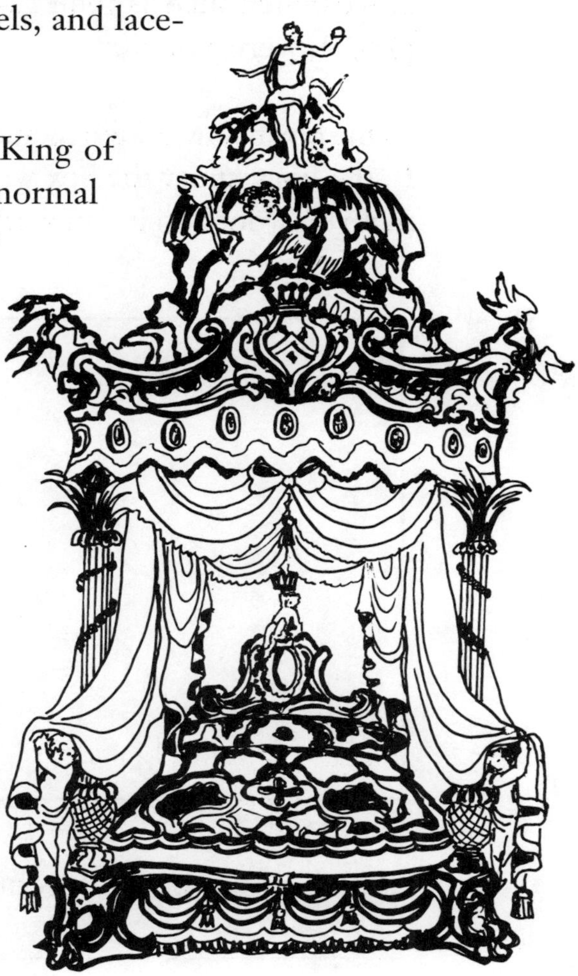

My morning Routine

Time	Activity~
	Get Up

A DAY IN THE LIFE OF LOUIS XIV 1643-1715

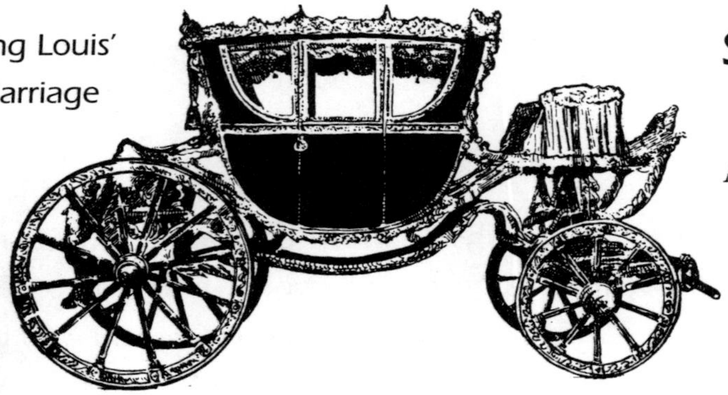

King Louis' Carriage

DAILY LIFE

STATE MATTERS

After King Louis was dressed for the day, he attended mass with his family and discussed matters of state in the Council Room of the palace. The Council Room had gilded moldings, huge mirrors, crystal chandeliers, and the magnificent paintings the king had personally selected. France was the most powerful nation in Europe at this time, and the king listened intently to the Foreign Secretary's report. King Louis believed that God himself had ordained him to be the King of France. He thought that Englishmen such as John Locke who believed that sovereignty belonged to the people, were absurd.

In the box below draw a picture of the king's council room as it has been described. In the lines under the box write a few sentences describing something important that you would do if you were the king or queen. Be creative.

Something important I would do as king or queen:

____

____

A DAY IN THE LIFE OF LOUIS XIV 1643-1715

FOOD

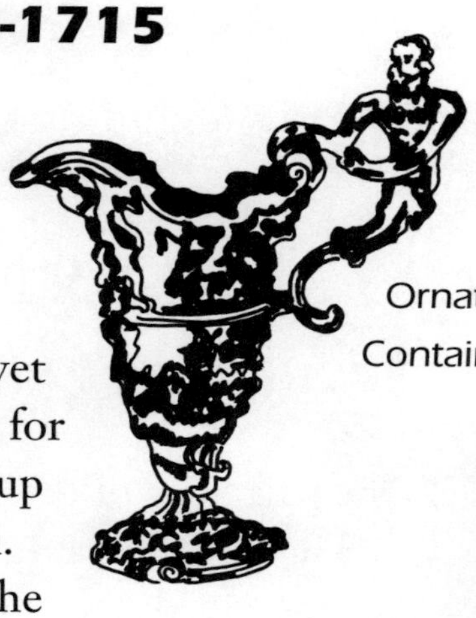

Ornate Container

DAILY LIFE

The king has many attendants at his royal luncheon, yet he chooses to eat in silence. Eating is serious business for King Louis XIV. He begins with several bowls of soup then devours partridge, pheasant, ham, and mutton. Next he has a salad to cleanse his palate. Finally, he enjoys cheese, fruit, and pastries. Louis prefers eating with his fingers though forks have just become popular. He wipes his fingers on a linen napkin because it is no longer proper to wipe ones fingers on the tablecloth. The king will have another lavish meal similar to his lunch at 10:00 at night, which he calls supper. His evening snack right before bedtime will consist of three small loaves of bread, cold meats, and two bottles of wine. (Is it any wonder that the autopsy on King Louis revealed a royal stomach twice the normal size?!)

On the lines below list 10 foods that you would choose to eat if you were king or queen and could choose any food you wanted.

Then decide which of the four food groups the food you chose is in. Remember, the four food groups are: the meat group, dairy group, breads and grains group, and fruits and vegetables group. Write your answer next to your food choice.

Choice of Food — Food Group

1. ______________________________
2. ______________________________
3. ______________________________
4. ______________________________
5. ______________________________
6. ______________________________
7. ______________________________
8. ______________________________
9. ______________________________
10. ______________________________

*B*AROQUE

ART

ITALIAN BAROQUE PAINTING:
Caravaggio

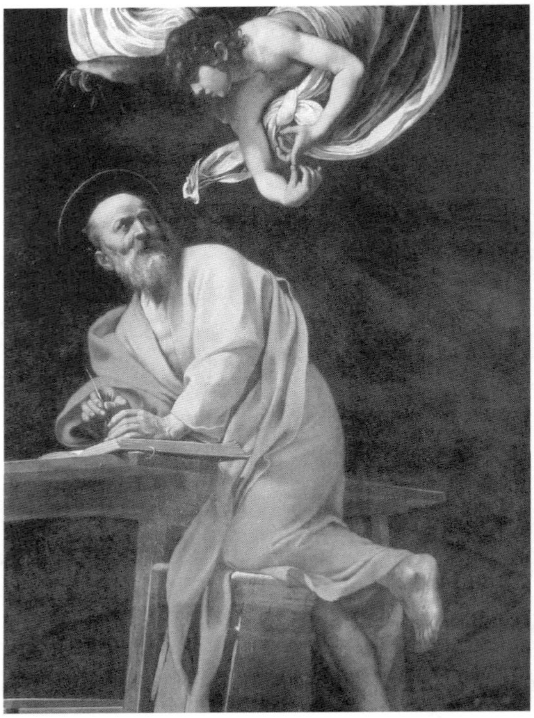

Caravaggio painting

The paintings of the Italian Michelangelo Merisi da Caravaggio (1573-1610) influenced nearly all artists of the Baroque period. His style is unique and recognizable by its strong lighting and dramatic effects.

Caravaggio's early art training was limited to study with a little-known pupil of the famous Venetian artist Titian. Caravaggio seemed to have had a natural art talent that exhibited itself early in his life. He enjoyed working directly from a model rather than making preliminary sketches. He made unparalleled use of *chiaroscuro* (key arrow SKEWR o) this means he used light and shadows as important compositional elements. He liked to paint fruit in its most realistic state, showing all the blemishes of rotting and signs of aging. He also liked to make dramatic use of perspective so that a hand might appear to be coming directly at you. Caravaggio was the painter whom all others artists of the period, including Rembrandt, used as an example.

Luckily they did not follow him in other ways. At least one of Caravaggio's tragic flaws was his monumentally bad temper. He easily flew into rages, became violent, and was unable to control himself. He died of a fever after one of his rages at the young age of 37.

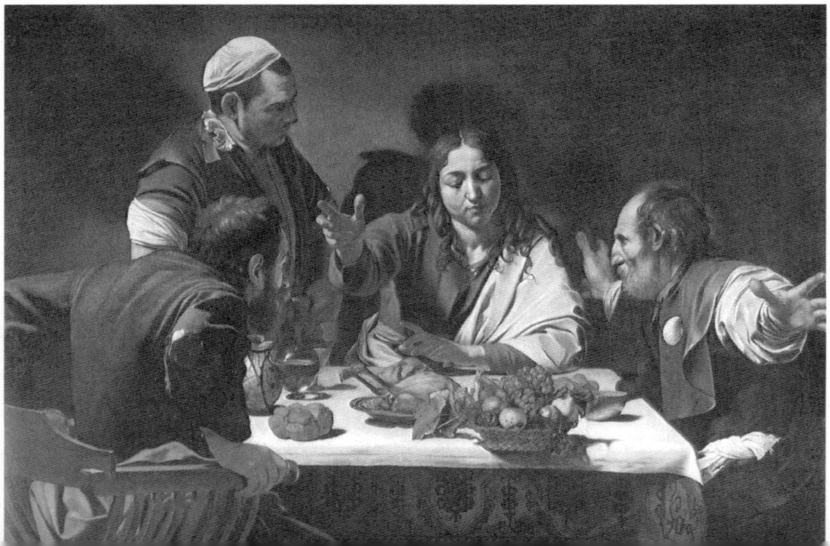

Caravaggio painting

Activity~

1. What Baroque characteristics are shown in the work of Caravaggio?

____

____

2. What were some of Caravaggio's tragic flaws?

____

____

____

____

3. Draw two bowls of fruit. Make one idealized, with gorgeous, perfect fruit. Draw the other as Baroque fruit, meaning realistic to a fault. Show rotten areas and insect damage.

Do you think the overly realistic fruit might have been a symbol for the way Caravaggio felt about his life or maybe about life in general? Explain.

____

____

____

____

____

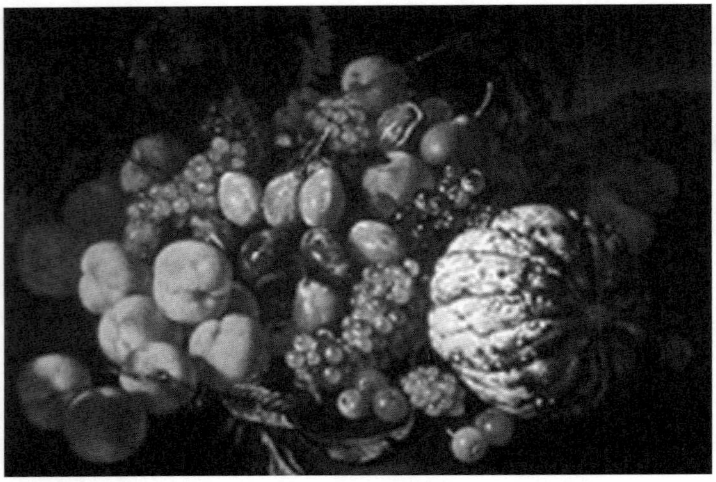

OBSERVING THE NATURAL WORLD

What Does Fruit Look Like?

Look closely at a piece of fruit. This is what Caravaggio and Giovan Battisa did. They saw all the flaws. What do you see? Describe the fruit in the spaces below.

ART

Adjectives

shape ______________________________

color ______________________________

texture ______________________________

other features ______________________________

Nouns

What is this fruit? ______________________________

____

Verbs

What can this fruit do? ______________________________

____

Similes

Use your imagination

This fruit is like a . . . ______________________________

____

Draw the fruit below.

BAROQUE POETRY WITH HAIKU STRUCTURE

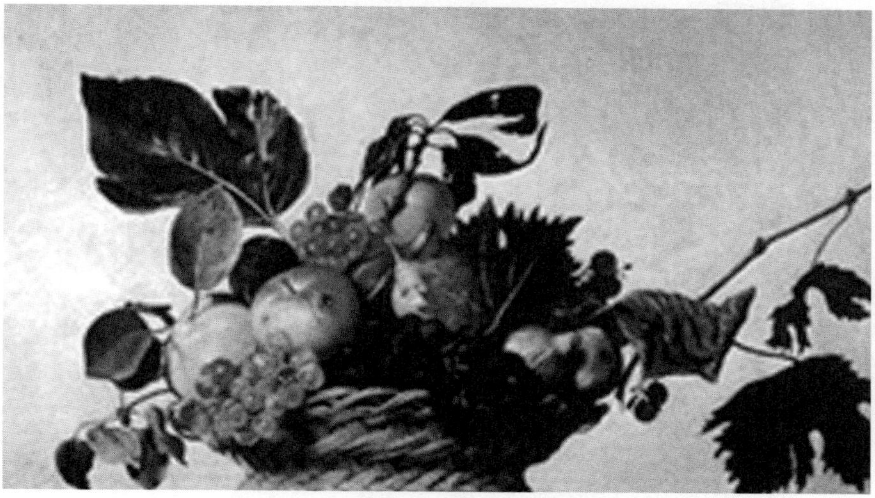

Haiku is a Japanese poetic structure with three lines and definite syllable counts for each line. Haiku is written to describe nature.

Figs, dates, apricots
Golden, red, purple and green.
A feast for the eyes.

ART

Look at the words on page 26 that you used to describe fruit and at drawings of the fruit. Using these ideas, write a three-line unrhymed poem in the spaces below. The required syllables for each line are marked in parentheses.

Fruit

____ (5)

____ (7)

____ (5)

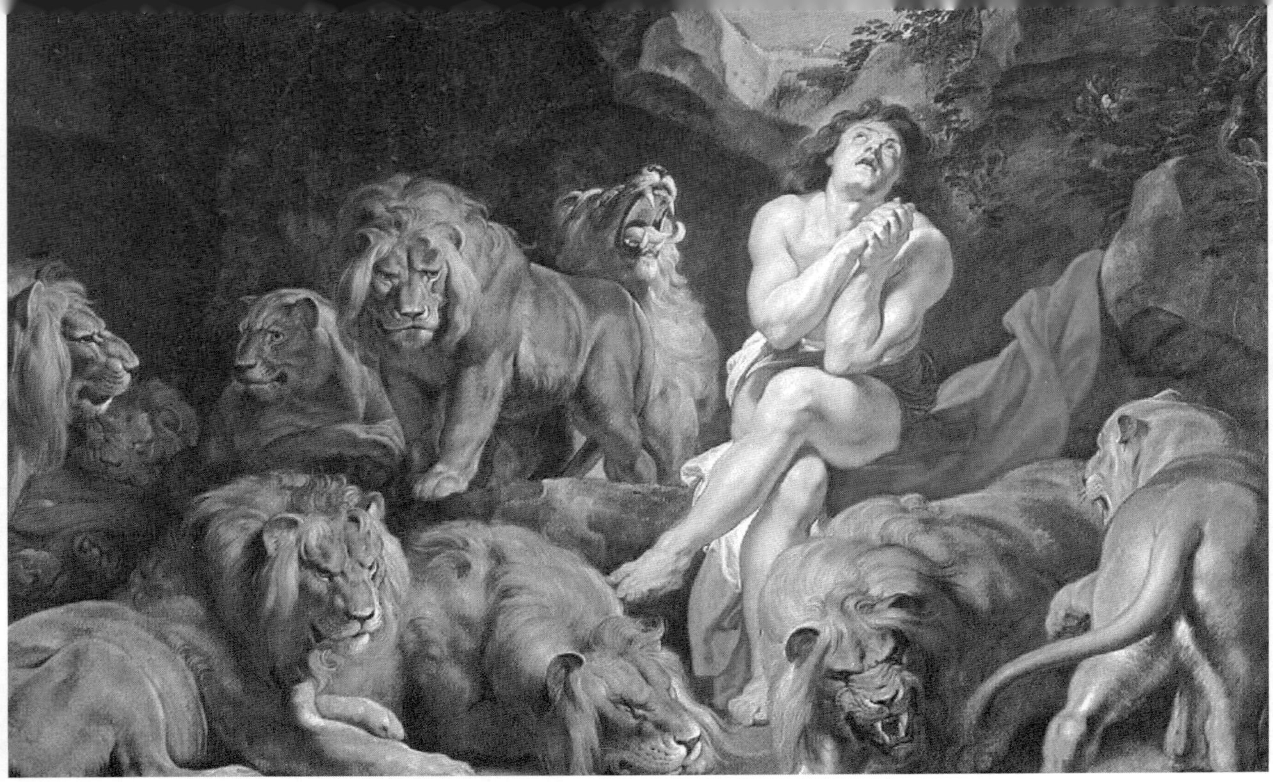

Ruben's DANIEL IN THE LION'S DEN

ART

OBSERVING THINGS

LET'S REALLY LOOK AT A PAINTING

Study Rubens' painting of *Daniel in the Lion's Den* carefully, then answer the following questions.

1. **Subjects** — check what you see

❑ animals ❑ buildings ❑ trees ❑ sky ❑ flowers
❑ adults ❑ children ❑ indoors ❑ outdoors ❑ food
❑ musical instruments ❑ transportation ❑ vehicles ❑ other

2. **Lines** — check what you see

❑ sharp ❑ curved ❑ choppy ❑ thick ❑ thin
❑ vertical ❑ horizontal ❑ diagonal ❑ jagged
❑ other

3. What **lines** are repeated the most?__________________________________

____

____

4. **Shapes** — check what you see

❑ circles ❑ squares ❑ rectangles ❑ triangles

5. What kind of **balance** is used?

❑ symmetrical (both sides of the painting are similar)
❑ asymmetrical (both sides of the painting are different)
❑ radial (subjects branch out like a wheel from a central point)

6. **Focal point** — What is the first thing you see in the painting?

____

____

ART

7. **Purpose** — check what you think is the artist's primary purpose.

❑ to imitate nature
❑ to express emotion
❑ to show a creative design

8. **Describing words** — check the words below that describe this painting.

❑ strength ❑ love ❑ excitement ❑ courage ❑ fear
❑ hope ❑ hate ❑ anger ❑ loneliness ❑ sadness
❑ peace ❑ death ❑ mystery ❑ happiness ❑ other

9. **Write a paragraph** — Study the painting one more time as well as your answers to the above questions. Then on a separate sheet of paper, write a paragraph describing this artwork and your reaction to it.

____

____

____

____

____

____

For more information about looking at paintings see *Smart Art* by Patricia Hollingsworth and Stephen Hollingsworth published by Zephyr Press.

Guido Reni
1575-1642

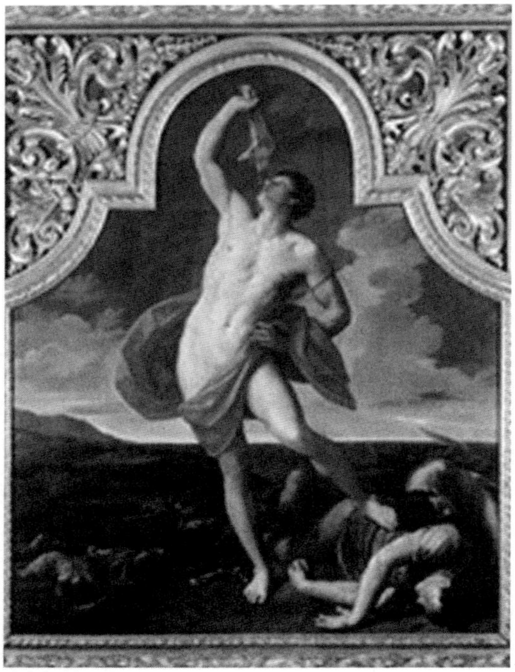

Reni's Victorious Samson

Like most Baroque painters, Guido Reni was strongly influenced by the work of Carravagio. Look carefully at Reni's painting of the *Victorious Samson*.

List many, varied, and unusual words to describe this painting.

____

____

Which of these words are also words that describe Baroque ideals?

____

____

____

ART

Artemesia Gentileschi
1593-1653

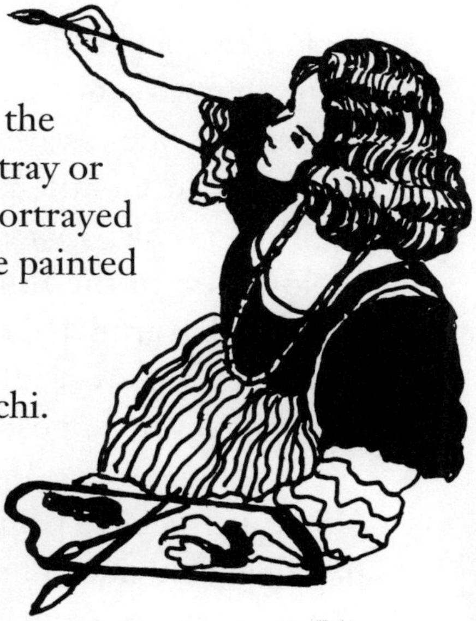

Artemesia Gentileschi

The Baroque era was a time of great change in the arts. While the goal of Renaissance art was to portray or show beauty, the art of the Baroque period portrayed emotion and excitement, everything seemed to be painted or sculpted on a grander scale.

One painter of this period was Artemesia Gentileschi. Gentileschi was the first woman of her time to be widely known and appreciated as an artist. She was born in Rome in 1593. Her father was an artist, so from an early age Artemesia was exposed to the arts and to many of the famous artists of her time. As a young girl, Gentileschi was educated at home, and her father gave her lessons in art. As she grew older, her father decided she needed more education, and because women were not allowed to enter art school, Artemesia's father arranged for her to be tutored by another artist Agostino Tassi.

Lessons with Tassi, under the watchful eye of a female chaperone, went well in the beginning. One day, however, something terrible happened. Tassi physically attacked Artemesia Gentileschi and hurt her very badly. Even though Tassi underwent a trial and spent eight months in jail, he was eventually declared not guilty. During the trial Artemesia was questioned and at one point even tortured by officials who tried to make her change her story.

After the trial Artemesia tried to go on with her life. She married a man from Florence, Pietro Antonio de Vincenzo Strattesi. After the marriage the couple lived in Florence, and there they had a daughter Palerma. Palerma would grow up to be an artist like her mother.

By the time she was 23, Gentileschi was an established artist. She was invited to join a group of important artists in Florence called the Academy. During the next ten years, she moved from Florence to Genoa to Venice. Her art was well received in these cities also. When Gentileschi was 37, she moved to Naples where she lived for the rest of her life.

ART

Artemesia began to be famous early in her career for her portraits. As she matured, the focus of her work changed dramatically. Perhaps it was the attack by her teacher or disappointment with her marriage, but Artemesia began to paint dramatic pictures of heroines from the Bible — Judith, Esther, and Bathsheba. She always painted pictures of the most intense or exciting part of the story. In Gentileschi's most famous painting, *Judith Beheading Holofernes*, Judith and her maidservant are shown cutting off the head of General Holofernes. In the Bible story, Judith is a woman who saves her village from the Assyrian army led by General Holofernes. Judith and her maid behead him with his own sword, then put the head in a basket and carry it to the enemy line. When the opposing army sees their general's head, they flee in terror.

Other artists have painted scenes from this story, but Gentileschi's painting is the most dramatic. The painting is nearly life-size, and the light on the subjects seems to come from a single source. The two women look as if they are struggling hard with the general. The scene is violent and terrifying.

Gentileschi painted two other pictures of Judith, each as detailed and active as the first.

By the time she turned 40, Gentileschi's style of painting was no longer popular. In order to make her living as an artist, she changed the way she painted pictures. She continued to paint Biblical scenes, but these were calmer, less emotional scenes, such as *David and Bathsheba.*

Artemesia Gentileschi lived to be 60 years old. She painted pictures and made her living as an artist for her entire life. We admire her not only for her artwork, but because she lived an eventful, challenging, and independent life for a woman of her time. Artemesia died in 1653, one of history's great artists.

Activity~

Imagine what it might have been like to be a female artist during the Baroque time. Write about your feelings and ideas. What subjects would you have painted?

ART

BAROQUE: ARTISTS

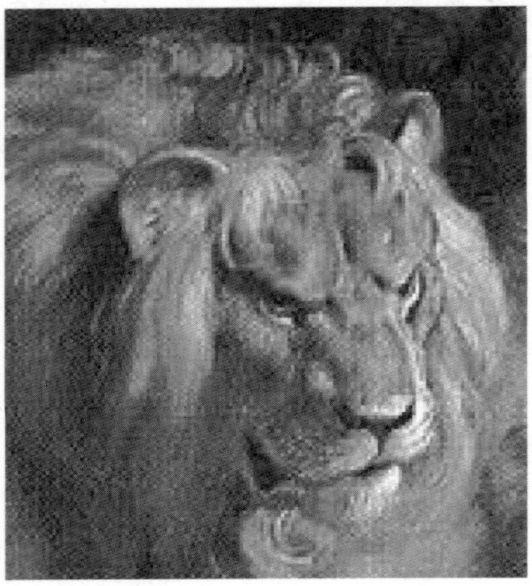

Ruben's lion

Artists in the Baroque era also studied nature. When they painted animals and people they made them dramatic and exciting. Some animals even seemed to be showing emotion. Compare Dürer's painting of a rabbit to the lions in Ruben's *Daniel in the Lion's Den*. Dürer's rabbit is painted in a calm realistic Renaissance manner while Ruben's lions exude emotion and excitement.

ART

Pretend that you are an artist in the Baroque time period. List many, various animals that you could paint.

____

____

____

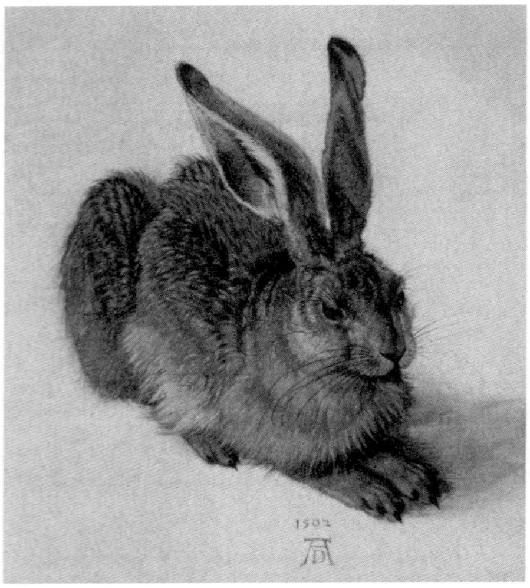

Dürer's rabbit

Now list unusual kinds of animals that you might paint.

____

____

____

Add to your list anything that comes to mind that you might like to paint along with your animal.

____

____

____

Now draw your animal!

Daniel in the Lion's Den

BY PETER PAUL RUBENS

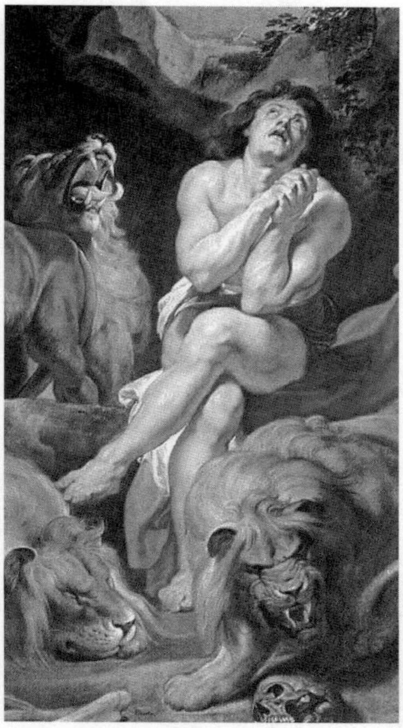

Ruben's Daniel

Unlike the Renaissance art which represented nature in a restrained manner, Baroque style added strong feelings and emotions. Peter Paul Ruben's (1577-1640) painting *Daniel and The Lion's Den* shows Baroque characteristics. The faces and bodies of both Daniel and the lions convey strong emotions. The painting also shows dramatic lighting on Daniel. There is also a feeling of movement, which is shown in the drapery, the lions' manes, tails and faces.

In order to paint this with emotion, Rubens had to imagine what it was like to be both the lion and Daniel. First, pretend that you are the lion. Move as though:
— you are stalking your prey
— you are awakening from a long sleep and stretching
— you are angry and growling
— you are frisky and playful
— you are devouring your dinner

Now pretend you are Daniel and are trapped in a hole. Use your hands to feel the walls. Look up at the light coming down from the ceiling. Hear the breath of the nearby lions and feel their fur brushing against your skin.

Study the painting and write a list of the many, varied feelings for:

The Lions____

____

____

Daniel ____

____

____

Writing Assignment

Using the five senses, make a list of many varied and unusual words to describe *Daniel and the Lion's Den.*

How would you describe the lions? How do they feel and look? What sounds would you hear? What do you think the lions are thinking? What do they smell? Write a paragraph using the list of words you wrote to describe the painting.

ART

Extension

Compare the list of words you used to describe Dürer's rabbit in the Renaissance with the list you made for Daniel and the lions. What do they have in common? How are they different?

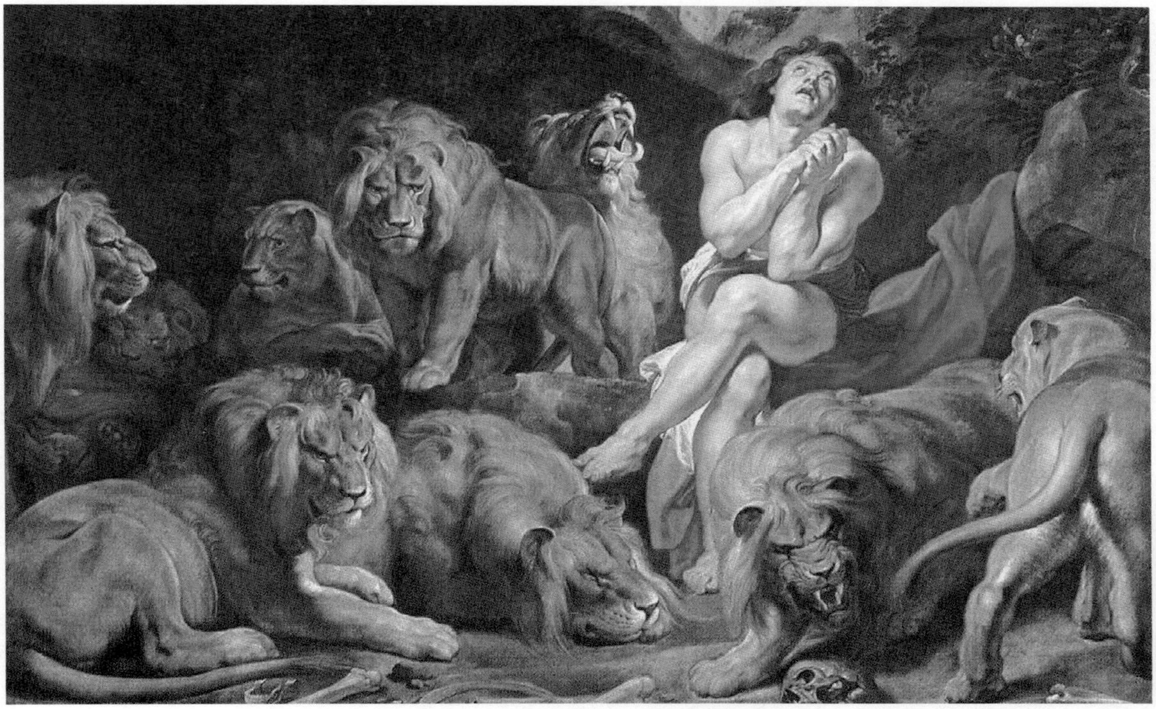

Ruben's DANIEL IN THE LION'S DEN

ART

DEFINITION POEM

1. Pick one word to describe *Daniel and the Lion's Den*. (Put it on the first and last line below.)

2. Now think of two short phrases (not sentences) that describe this word. Write them on the lines in between.

EXAMPLE:	YOUR WORDS:
Help	______________________
Scared beyond words	______________________
Shaking with fear	______________________
Help	______________________

3. Guess what? You just wrote a poem!

Velásquez: 1656

The Maids of Honor

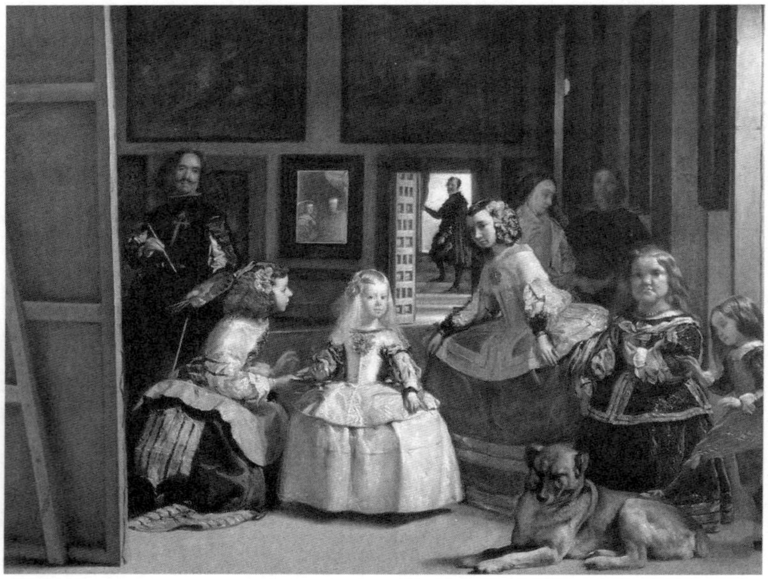

Velásquez's Maids of Honor

The Maids of Honor (Las Meninas in Spanish), a great and interesing work of art, is set in Velásquez's studio. The focal point of the painting is the little Spanish Princess Margarita dressed in her finery. With her are two attendants and two dwarfs. The dwarfs were used by royalty as both playmates and attendants for children.

On the left of the painting is a self-portrait of Velásquez as he is witnessing and painting the scene on the large canvas in front of him. Dimly in the backgound you can see a mirror that shows that the king and queen are viewing this domestic scene from the same vantage point that you and I are looking at it.

ART

Activity~

Draw a picture of yourself in your home. Make yourself the focal point.

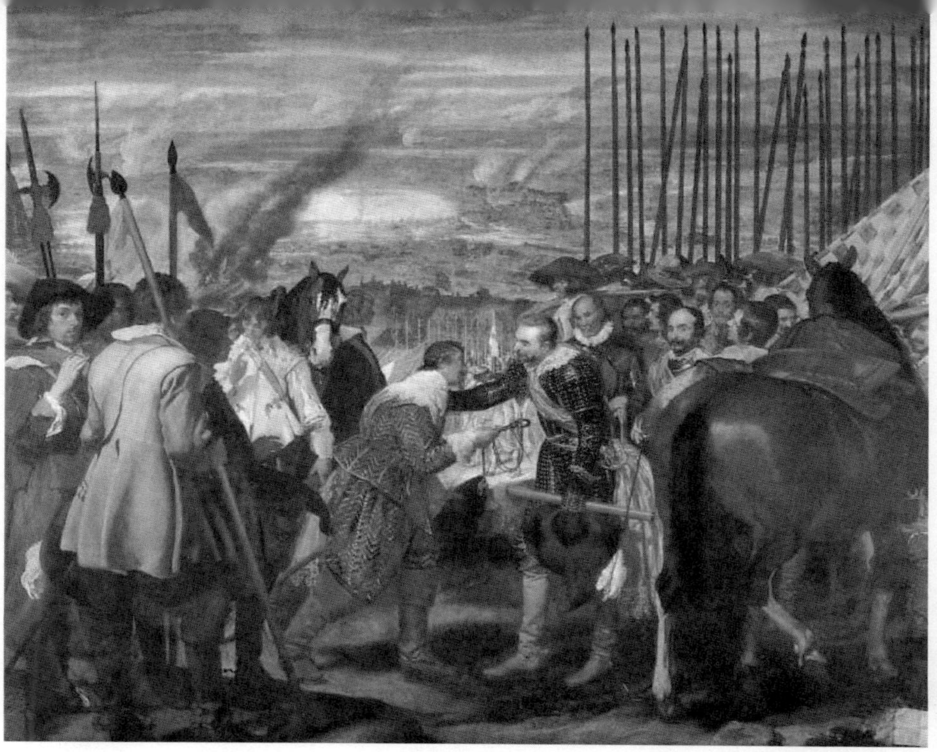

Velásquez's
SURRENDER OF BREDA

ART

VELÁSQUEZ: PAINTER OF HISTORY

Velásquez's painting *The Surrender of Breda* shows the 1625 victory of Spain over the Dutch. Velásquez's portrayal of this event gives you an idea of what people actually wore during the Baroque time period in Spain.

Activity~

Make a drawing of what leaders today wear when they meet.

Diego Velásquez

Diego Velásquez was the painter for Spanish kings and queens during much of the Baroque time period. His broad and direct brushstrokes had a strong influence on the Impressionist painter Manet. The modern art master Pablo Picasso was also influenced by Velásquez, particularly the most famous of Velásquez's works *The Maids of Honor*.

ART

Activity~

Draw the Princess Margarita from page 38 using only geometric shapes such as circles, triangles, squares and rectangles. Your picture will look somewhat like a Picasso.

DUTCH ARTISTS

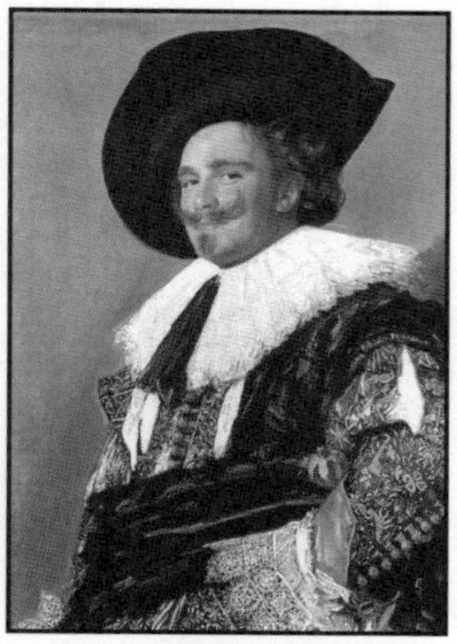

Hals' Painting

Dutch is the term used for people who lived in Holland (now known as the Netherlands.) At least three masterful artists lived there during the Baroque time period. They and other artists provided artwork for the wealthy, emerging Dutch middle class. Their artwork experimented with the use of light and the expression of a moment in time.

Frans Hals
1581-1666

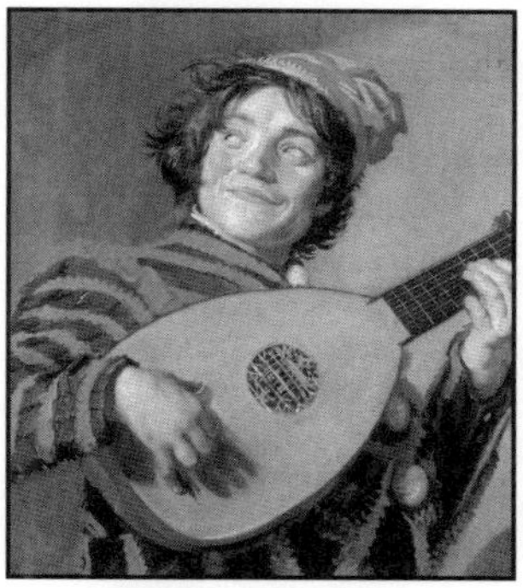

Hals' LUTE PLAYER

Frans Hals (1581-1666) is most known for painting joyous and glorious portraits of ordinary people. His portraits are lively, exciting, and painted with beautiful, bold brush strokes. He influenced later artists such as Manet and the Impressionists.

ART

Activity~

Make drawings of ordinary people having a good time.

Jan Vermeer 1632-1675

Vermeer lived in Delft with his wife, mother-in-law, and eleven children. It is little wonder that his subjects were most often painted in quiet, contemplative moods. He is an artist who sought tranquility in work. Usually the only action in Vermeer's paintings is sunlight coming through a window. His art captures the beauty found in ordinary human households.

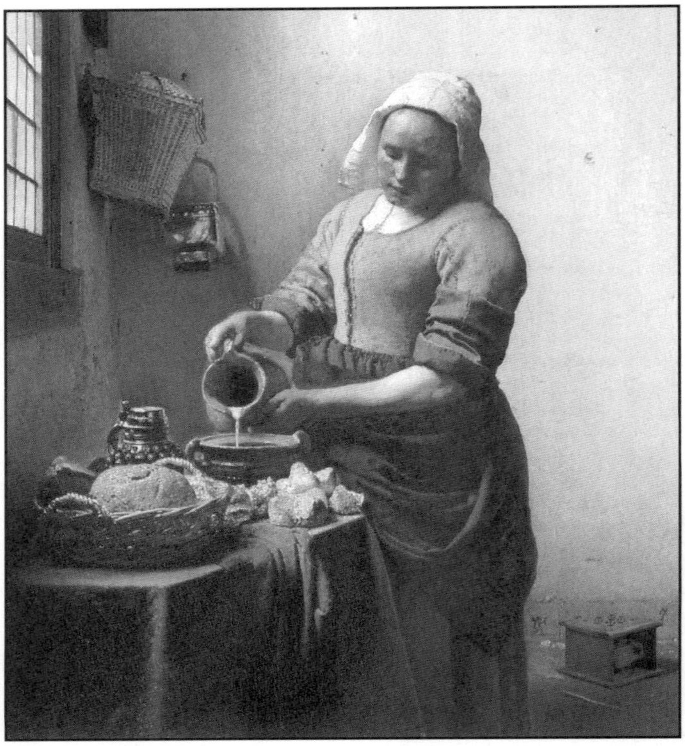

Vermeer's MILK MAID

ART

Activity~

Make drawings of things you see in your room or your house.
Be sure your drawings are calm, like Vermeer's.

Rembrandt Van Rijn
1606-1669

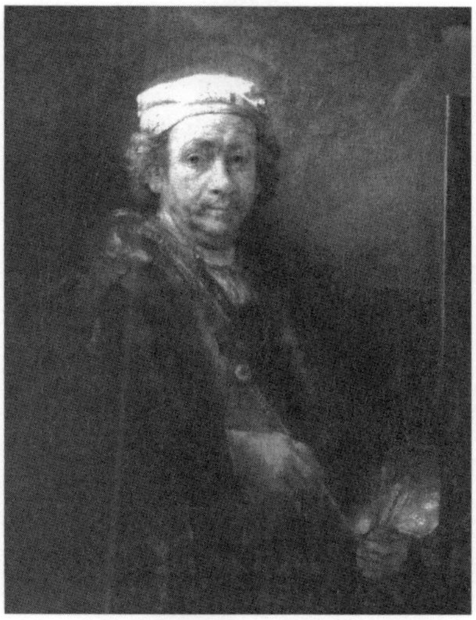

Rembrandt's self portrait

Rembrandt is one of the world's best and most famous artists. His life began in an ordinary way for someone who lived in that time.

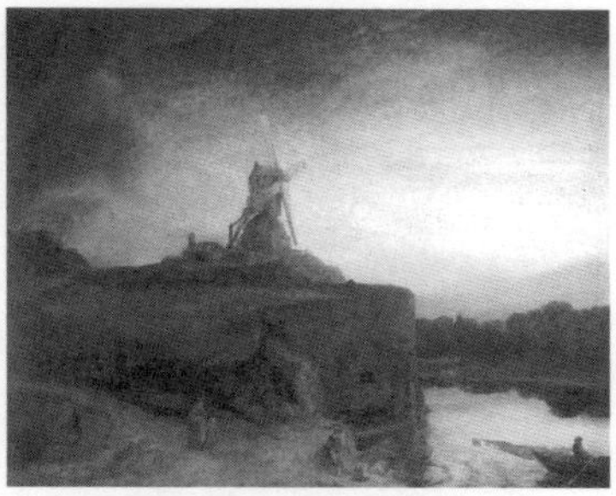

Rembrandt's WINDMILL

The windmill is commonly associated with the Dutch landscape. The windmill, with its great grinding stone, was the chief tool for a miller to turn wheat into flour. One miller's son was the famous artist Rembrandt.

ART

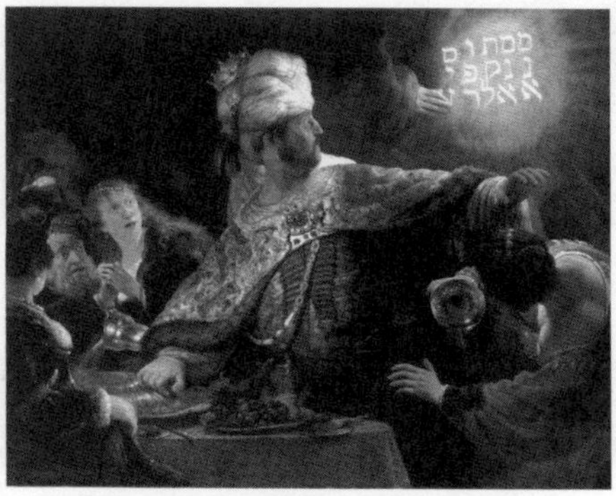

Dramatic Rembrandt

Rembrandt painted landscapes with windmills, ordinary people, and Biblical scenes, but most often he experimented with his own portrait. These self-portraits were like laboratory experiments in showing character through the human face. Rembrandt used dramatic lighting and *chiaroscuro* (key arrow SWEWR 0). This means he used light and shadow for compositional purposes.

Activity~

Make two dramatic self-portraits using different expressions and *chiaroscuro*. If you use a pencil to draw, you can create shadows by using the side of the pencil lead.

REMBRANDT'S PORTRAITS

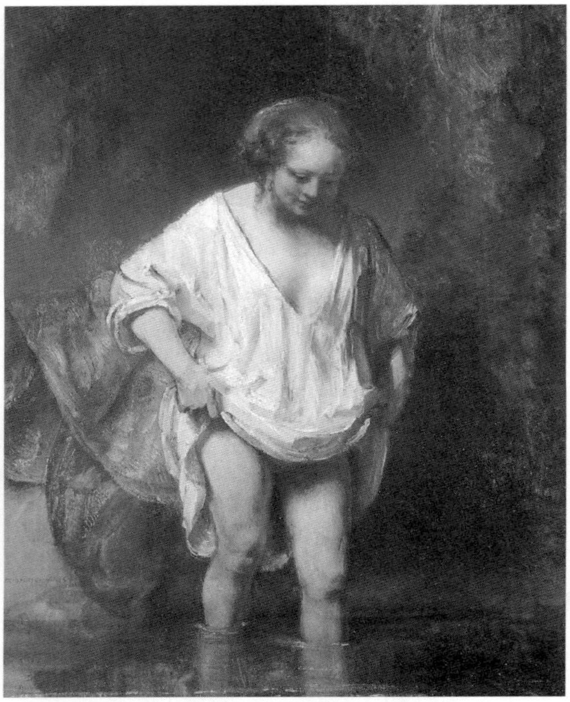

Rembrandt's wife

Rembrandt was renowned for painting portraits that revealed something of the character of the people being painted. He painted people in wonderfully dramatic lighting that seemed to capture their personalities. Look at the loving way Rembrandt portrayed his wife in *Hendrickje Bathing in a River*.

ART

Activity~

Imagine that you are swimming or wading in a river. Write sentences describing the way the water looks and feels, how it sounds, and what aromas might be in the air.

____

____

____

____

____

____

REMBRANDT'S GROUP PORTRAITS

Rembrandt often did groups of painting such as the one for *The Syndics of the Clothmaker's Guild*. Here you can distinctly see each person's face which is exactly what they wanted. After all, each person had paid for a portion of the portrait.

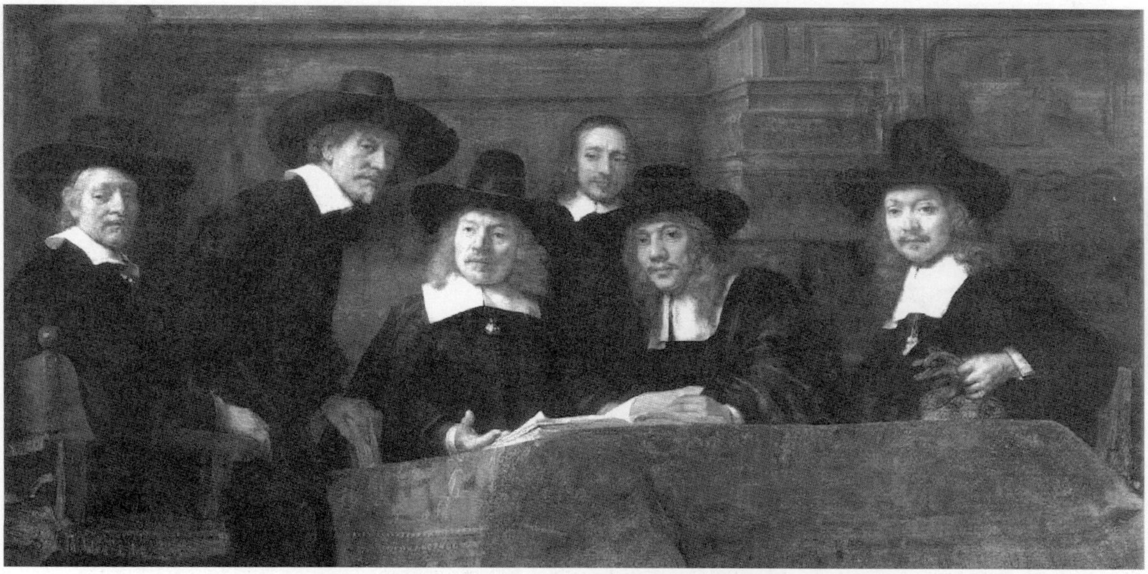

Rembrandt's CLOTHMAKER'S GUILD

ART

Activity~

Make a drawing of you and your friends.

REMBRANDT'S NIGHT WATCH

When the nightwatchmen hired Rembrandt they thought each person's face would show distinctly as in his previous portraits. This painting was for the new meeting hall of the Frans Banning Cocq. These were important men who defended the city in times of emergency.

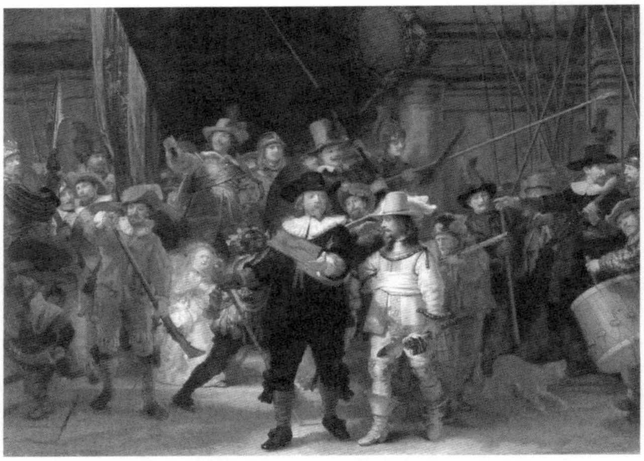

Rembrandt's NIGHT WATCH

ART

Rembrandt, who had seen and painted many group portraits for club halls, wanted to do something different. He wanted to create an interesting composition. While some people liked the painting, many of the men were outraged when they saw this painting because not every face is clearly shown.

Activity~

Imagine that you are unhappy with the way Rembrandt has painted you or your father. Write a letter to Rembrandt explaining your dissatisfaction.

Dear Mr. Rembrandt,

____

____

____

____

____

BE AN ARTIST

COMPARE

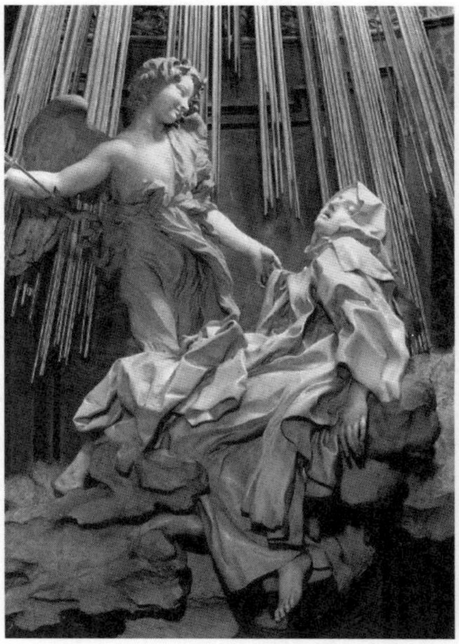

Bernini's Dramatic Baroque

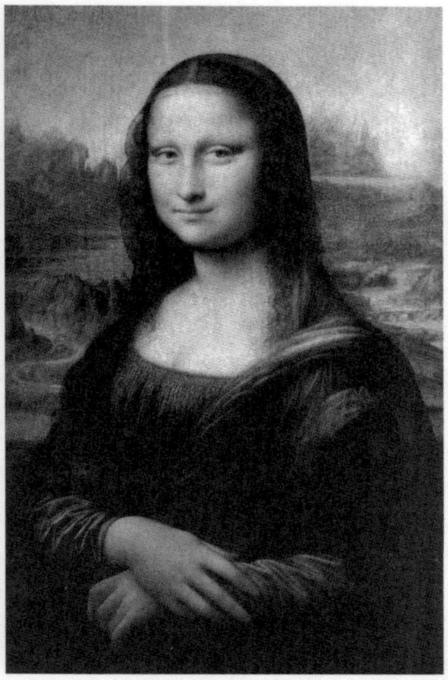

Leonado's Calm Renaissance

Renaissance artists were often scholars as well as artists. Many studied anatomy and nature to better portray people and animals. Their paintings and sculptures were calm, life-like, and restrained. Baroque artists chose to portray their subjects with a dramatic, emotional style. They would use *chiaroscuro*, a technique of using light and dark colors in a painting to produce a dramatic effect.

Activity~

Think about each style of work. Which style do you prefer? Draw a portrait in the style you prefer.

BAROQUE ART – 1600 AD TO 1700 AD

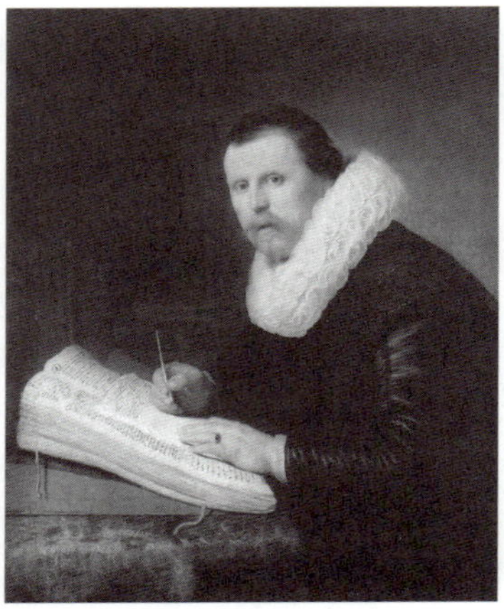

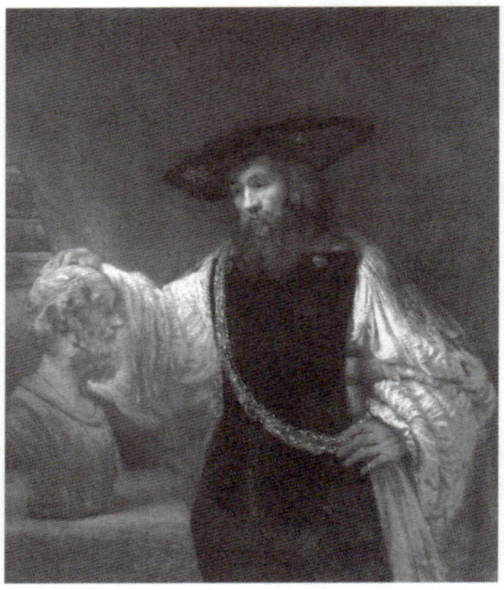

Rembrandt primarily painted people, which caused him to have a great interest in human character and personality. Some of Rembrandt's paintings have the dramatic lighting of Baroque art but not the dramatic facial expressions and movements.

ART

Activity~

Look carefully at these paintings by Rembrandt. Select one and write about what this person might be thinking.

Opulance and Ostentation

Baroque architecture is typified by Louis XIV's (1638-1715) palace in Versailles, France. It is the ultimate in opulence and ostentation. Its hundreds of rooms are decorated with gold, velvet, crystal, marble, and silver.

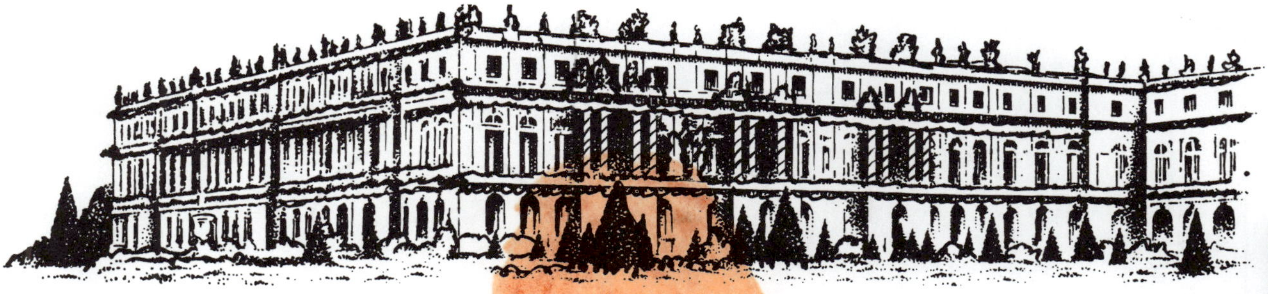

Palace of Versailles

Sir Christopher Wren's (1632-1723) masterpiece is St. Paul's Cathedral in London. Though classified as Baroque, it is one of the most classical, serene, and majestic of all Baroque architecture. It is solid, symmetrical, and monumental. The dome is 365 feet high, which is longer than a football field.

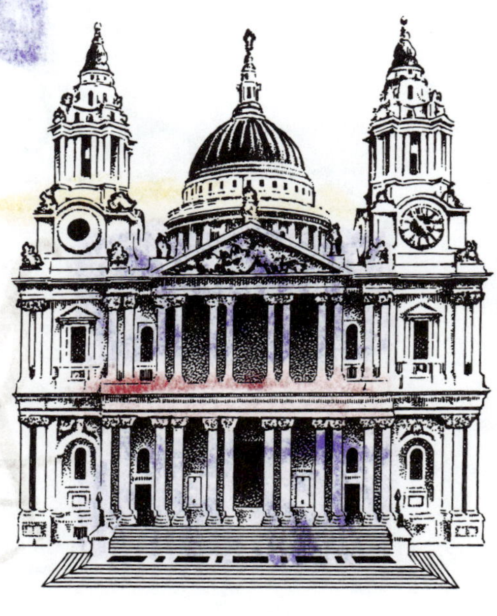

St. Paul's Cathedral

Activity~

Combine these two Baroque styles to design a building. Begin with the simple, solid design below and add more traditionally Baroque elements such as ovals, swirls, and elaborate decorations.

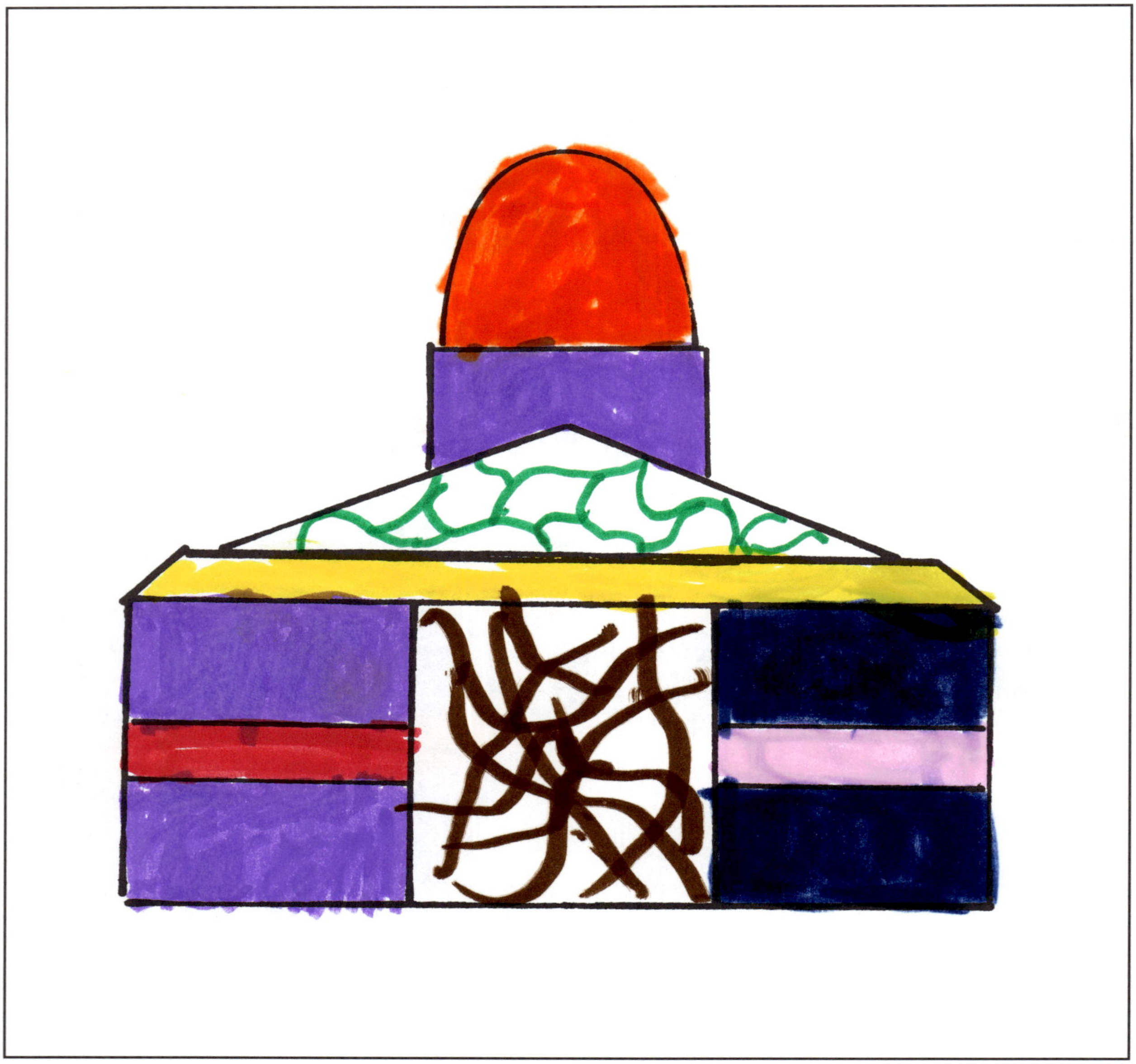

ARCHITECTURE

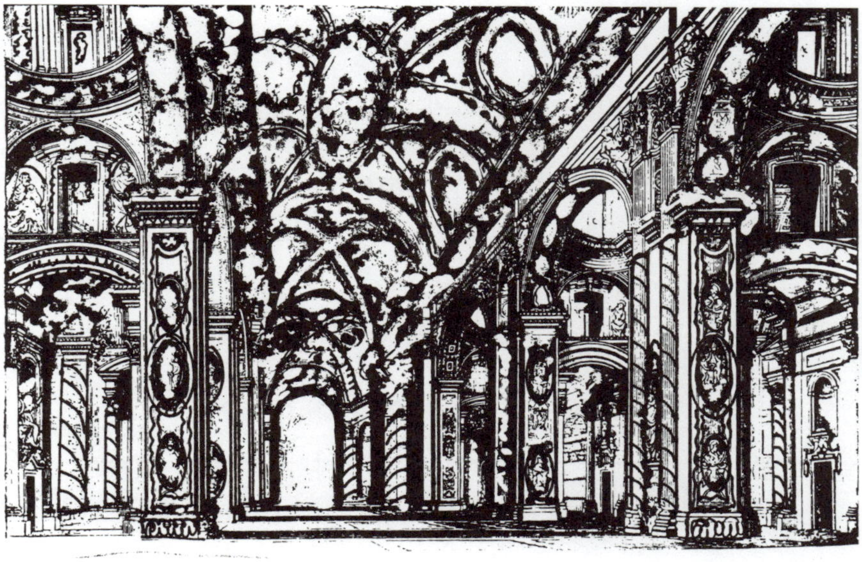

Grand Scale

Artists in the Baroque period worked on a grand scale. That means they created huge works of art that would not fit through a regular doorway. They loved to use brilliant colors and an abundance of objects in their paintings.

ARCHITECTURE

Imagine that you have been choosen to paint a wall or ceiling at your school. Make preparations as if you plan to paint it. Think of your auditorium, gymnasium, or maybe even the ceiling in your homeroom.

1. Write a sentence describing what you are planning to do.

____

2. List the materials and equipment you will need.

___________ ___________ ___________ ___________
___________ ___________ ___________ ___________
___________ ___________ ___________ ___________

3. What steps will you need to take — first, second, and third?

1. ________________ 3. ________________ 5. ________________
2. ________________ 4. ________________ 6. ________________

4. List any problems that you might encounter while you are working on your masterpiece.

____

____

5. Predict what the outcome will be. What will your painting be called?

____

____

6. Draw your design.

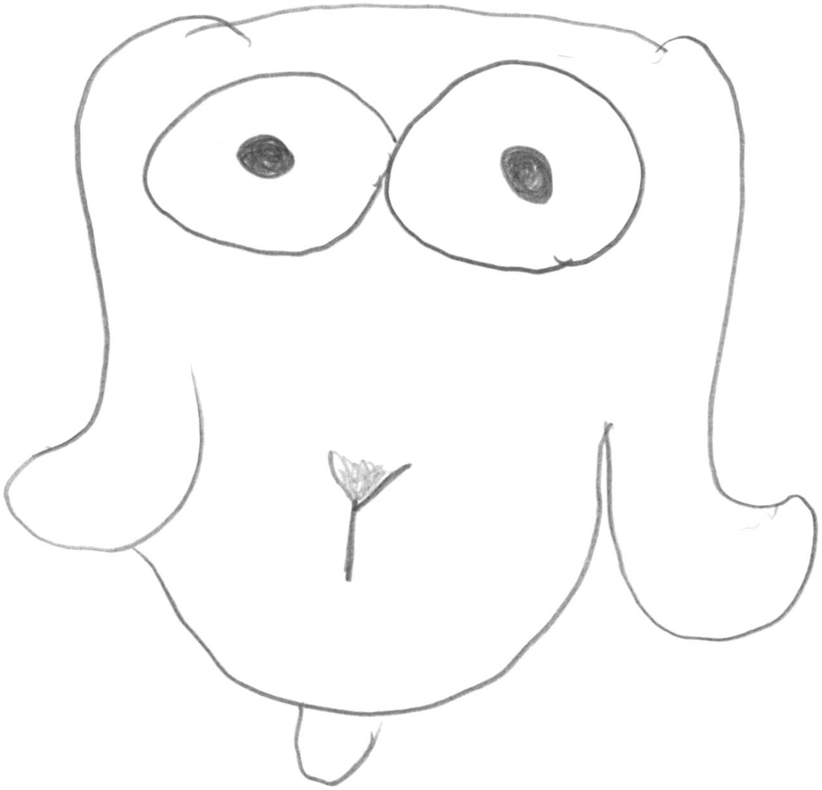

Ceiling Painting

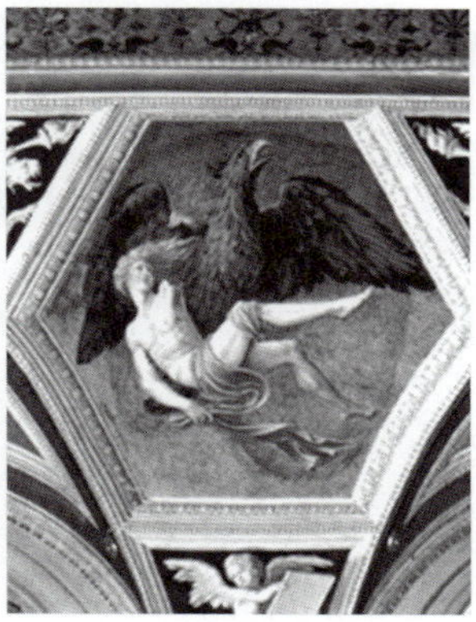

In the 17th century, a style of art known as Baroque was developed. It was well suited for large-scale pictures, as you would find in a church or palace. There was a lot of demand for this type of work in Roman Catholic countries such as Italy, Flanders, and Spain.

Painted ceilings were very fashionable at this time. The artists painted so cleverly that from the ground the stone structures looked real and the figures appeared to be floating through the air. These oval-shaped paintings would be of angels, clouds, and other elaborately decorative objects.

Activity~

Draw your own elaborately ornate Baroque ceiling within the shapes below.

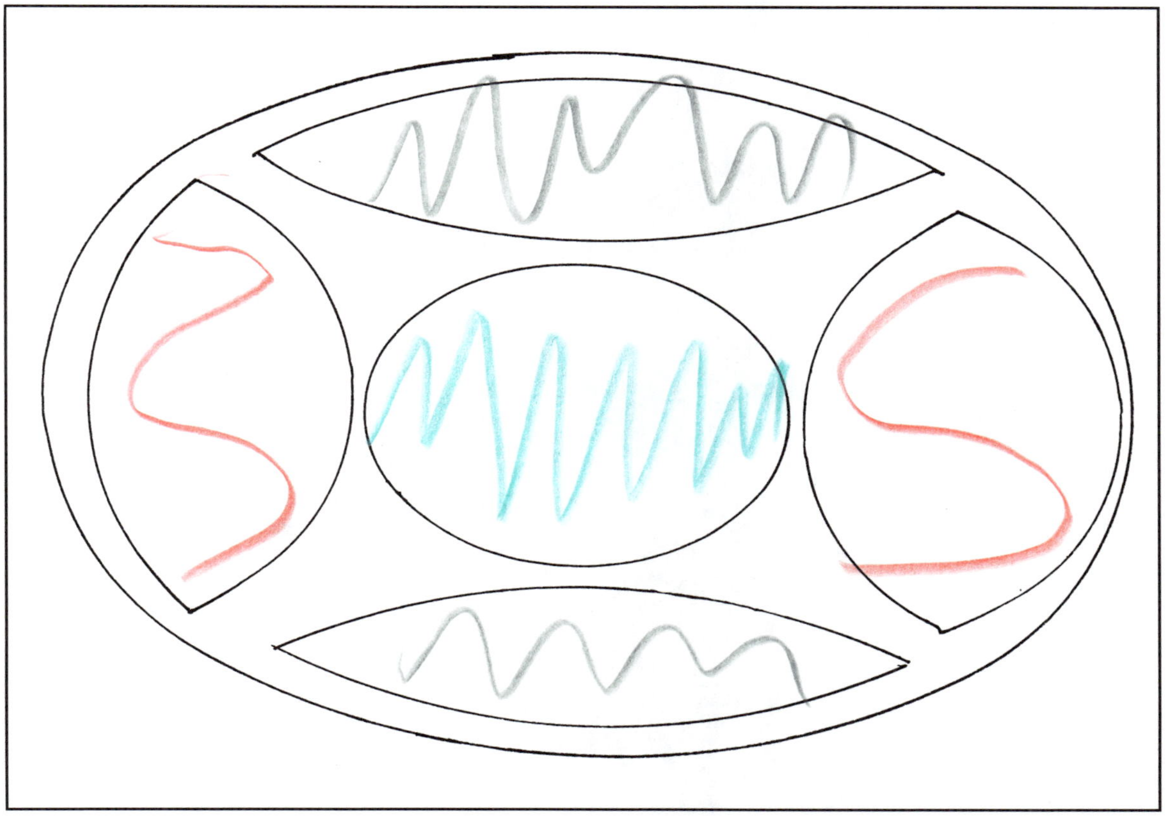

Activity~

List all the materials and equipment you will need. Then, list in order all the steps needed to complete the project. Finally, list the problems that might keep you from completing this project.

Imagine that you have been commissioned to paint the ceiling you designed.

1. What is the name of your ceiling painting?____________________________

2. What materials will you need?______________________________________

____

3. List all the steps you will need to take to complete the project?__________

____

4. What problems might arise?____

____

ARCHITECTURE

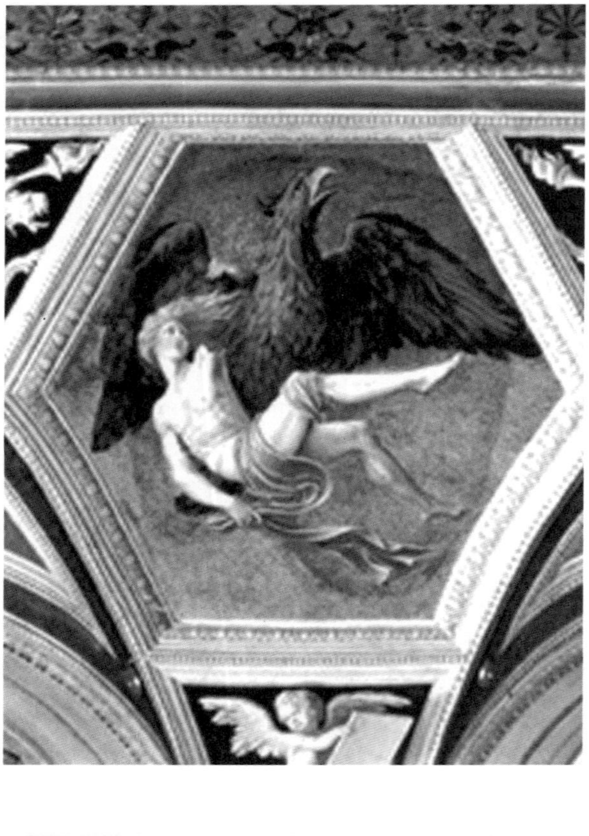

Greek and Roman Influence

Renaissance buildings, as well as paintings and sculpture, were influenced by the ancient Greeks and Romans. Renaissance builders revived the use of domes, columns, and rounded arches that had been abandoned during Medieval times. During the Baroque period, the emphasis was on dramatic, emotional art and architecture. The buildings were adorned with twisted columns, curlicues, oval windows, and other decorations. Below is a typical Renaissance building. Add the architectural features that would be seen in a Baroque building.

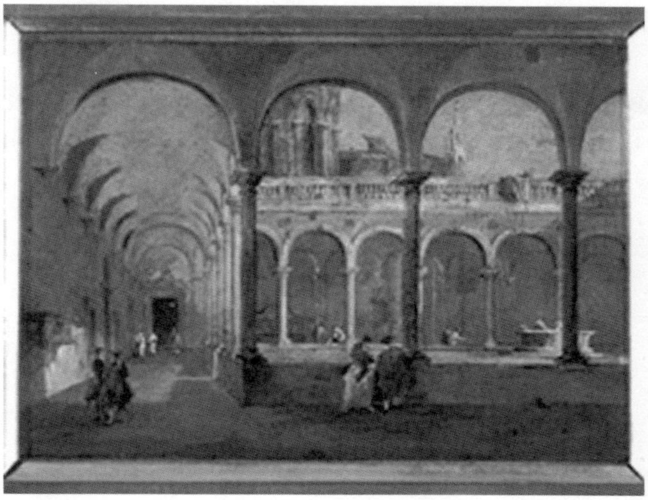

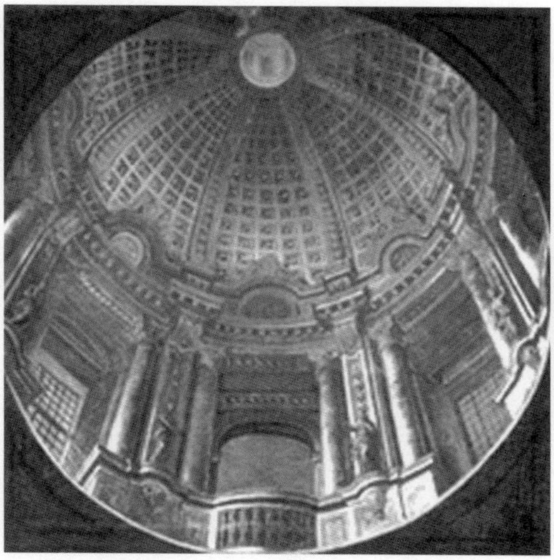

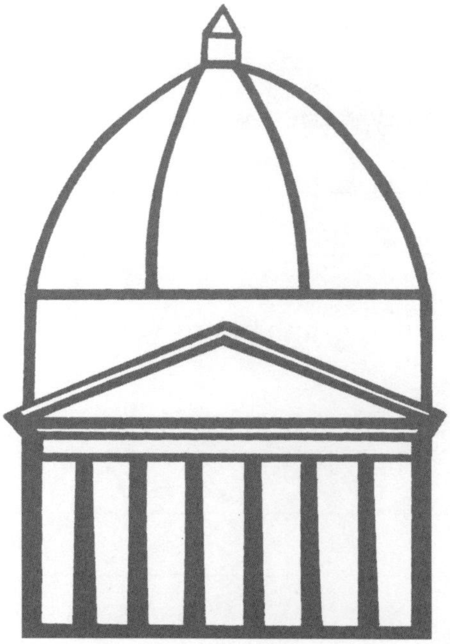

Decorated in Excess

The Baroque style contrasts sharply with the simplicity and balance of the Renaissance style. It looks as though Baroque architects took the Renaissance style as a cake to be decorated. Simple and elegant Renaissance columns became twisted like sticks of candy. Ovals surrounded by curlicues encompassed gold-drenched clouds, saints, angels, and cherubs as they moved and swirled on every surface. The Baroque style seems to say there can never be too much decoration.

Activities~

1. Draw a picture of your Baroque-style home.

2. Make a list of many, varied words to describe your Baroque home.

3. Write a poem or paragraph about your Baroque home using those descriptive words.

Dramatic Music

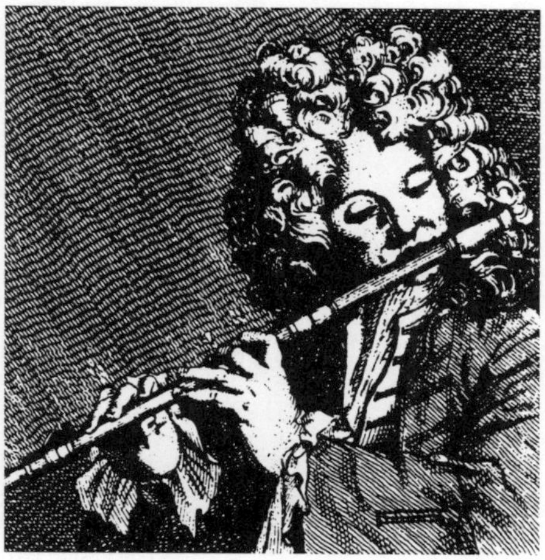

As with the architecture and art of the day, music in the Baroque period was dramatic, ornamented, emotional — and often excessive. The word *baroque*, probably from the Portuguese word meaning irregularly shaped pearl, was not necessarily a complimentary term initially. Because some took excesses to extremes, by the end of the Baroque period, people were so sick of the style that the term Baroque was associated with bad taste and shoddy workmanship. However, when we look back with 20th century eyes, we find magnificent examples of art, architecture, and some of the most beautiful music ever written.

Musical development during the Baroque period made great strides forward because of successes in scientific inquiry in the fields of physiology, astronomy, mathematics, and physics. Methods of inquiry in science sparked an interest in applying these methods to problems in music. One contribution to music from science is the development of a tempered (or well-tuned) scale. In nature, not all relationships between tones are the same distance apart. Using math and physics, the octave is divided into the twelve equal tones we still use today.

Baroque musicians were supported in several ways: by the Catholic church, by the aristocracy, and by wealthy merchants.

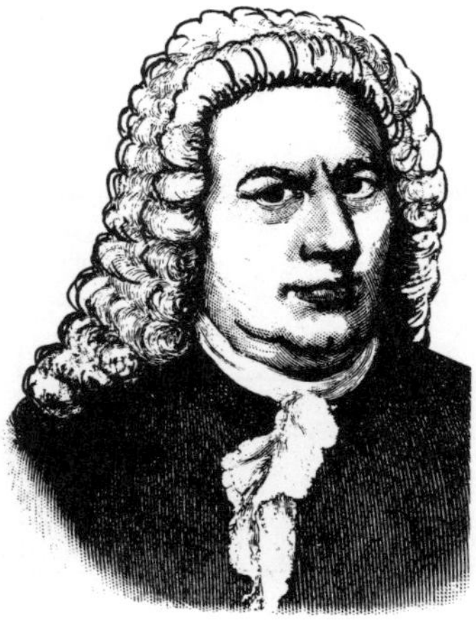

Churches hired musicians and commissioned composers to provide music for worship services and ceremonies such as weddings and funerals. The position usually included the job as church organist and choirmaster to choirs often made up mostly of young boys. Johann Sebastian Bach was a famous composer who was supported by the church.

Absolute monarchs in the form of kings or queens headed European governments. Courts of kings, princes, and other members of the aristocracy supported musicians who supplied music for entertainment, special occasions or ceremonies, and dances. A composer was usually kept employed full time at the court and was responsible for writing music according to the wishes of his patron. A famous court composer was George Frederick Handel.

A wealthy merchant class existed because of the successful European colonization of other parts of the world. Independent cities, such as Venice and Florence, had famous theaters where opera was developed and performed. These operas were often based on ancient Greek and Roman mythology. The elaborate stage machinery in the sets of these operas, as well as highly ornamented and dramatic solos (called arias in opera), were often of Baroque excess. Famous composers of Baroque opera were Monteverdi, Vivaldi, and Lully.

Activity~

Research the composers listed above. Find at least one piece of music written by each. Make a chart showing the name of the composer, the name of the piece of music, the type of music the piece is (opera, oratorio, orchestral, etc.), the type of instruments that usually perform it, and the year it was written.

COMPOSER	NAME OF MUSIC	TYPE OF MUSIC	INSTRUMENTS
Monteverdi			
Vivaldi			
Lully			

Musical Decoration

Baroque music is highly decorative. This decoration, called ornamentation in music, originated from performers improvising the ornaments (making up the ornaments in the music as they played) and continued developing into a tradition of expected ornaments. Some ornaments originating in the Baroque period are:

☐ **Trills:** rapidly moving back and forth between two consecutive notes

☐ **Mordents:** moving back and forth between two notes only one time.

☐ **Cadenzas:** section of rapidly moving notes inserted near the end of a piece of music that shows off the performer's mastery of his instrument.

☐ **Tremolo:** moving rapidly back and forth between two notes that are fairly far apart, such as a 4th.

☐ **Pizzicato:** stringed instrument technique of plucking strings instead of bowing.

☐ **Terraced dynamics:** sudden dramatic shifts in dynamics (volume); a section would be played at one volume level, such as loud, followed by a section played at soft volume level.

☐ **Word painting:** showing nonmusical ideas in the music; for example, singing about heaven might be accompanied by a bit of music rapidly going up.

Activity~

1. Draw a logo for each ornament in the box beside it.
2. Ask a musician to demonstrate how each of these ornaments are performed. Ask them to write down how they are notated in written music.

Instruments

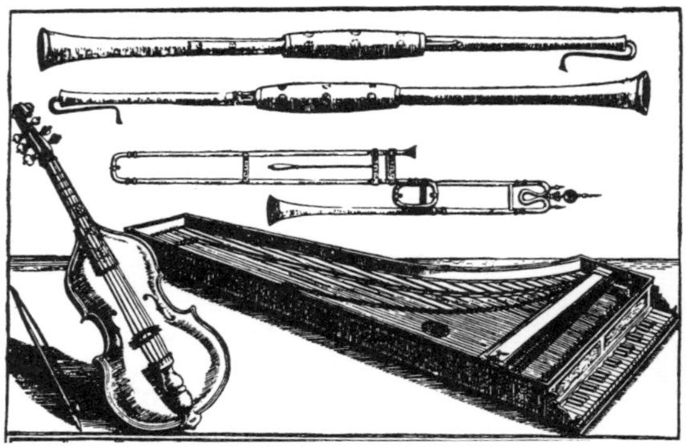

For the first time in musical history, composers began to name specific instruments to play specific parts in their compositions. Before this time, whatever instruments were available in the range of the music were used to play it.

Many of the instruments commonly used in the Baroque period are not regularly used today. Clavier was a term used for all types of keyboard instruments, including the harpsichord, the clavichord, the virginal, and the spinet. The harpsichord is a keyboard instrument whose strings are plucked with a quill, producing a charming tinkling sound. The recorder was used regularly in the Baroque orchestra. It is taught in many elementary schools today, although it rarely appears in modern orchestrations. The chalumeau and the hautbois were wind instruments commonly used in the Baroque era. The clarino or clarion, a high brass instrument, was used for many Baroque solos. The organ was smaller than our present organ and was unable to crescendo (gradually get louder). The string family was perfected during the Baroque period.

Activity~

Many of the instruments used in the Baroque were forerunners to modern-day instruments. List the instruments mentioned above. Using a reference book such as a dictionary, list the modern instruments that developed from these instruments.

____

____

____

____

Musical Forms and Styles

The Baroque period added many new forms of music.

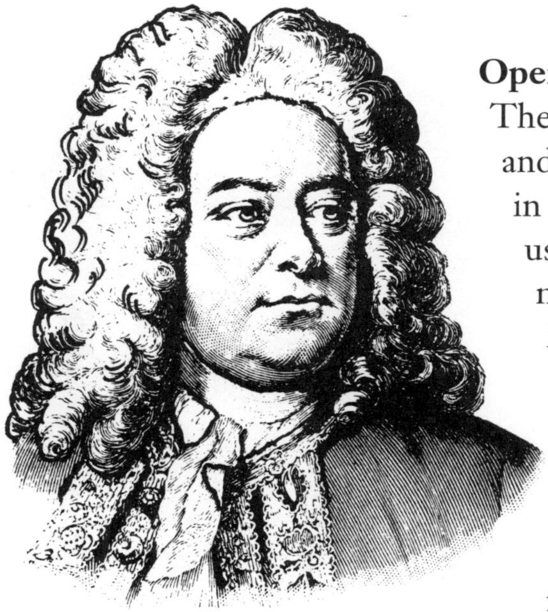

George Frederick Handel

Opera originated during the Baroque period. Theater, drama, poetry, acting, dance, costume, and scenery all come together in opera. Dialogue in opera is sung, not spoken. Subject matter usually came from Greek and Roman mythology. *Orfeo* by the Italian composer Monteverdi is an example of a Baroque opera with a mythological theme.

The **oratorio** is the Catholic church's version of opera. Instead of mythology, the subject matter of an oratorio comes from stories from the Bible. Oratorio involves less drama and acting and uses a narrator and a simpler set, usually the front of the church. The Baroque oratorio *The Messiah*, written by George Frederick Handel, is still performed regularly.

The **toccata**, sometimes called the prelude, is a form of music that has an improvised style and shows off the technical ability of the performer. The toccata is often paired with a fugue that is similar to a round or canon. One instrument begins with a theme, and that theme is imitated by two or more other instruments or groups of instruments. These imitations are not usually exact, but may be changed as the composer wishes. Listen to J.S. Bach's *Toccata and Fugue in d minor*. Awesome!

The **concerto grosso** consists of a small solo group of instruments and the full orchestra. The small solo group is featured and the rest of the orchestra accompanies. This is the most important form of concerto in the Baroque period. Any one of Bach's six *Brandenburg Concertos* is a good example of the concerto grosso.
A unique feature of the Baroque period is the use of **basso continuo**, which means that a bass line plays constantly to provide a continuous foundation for the music. The composer would simply write a bass line, and the performer

would improvise the chord structure on top of the bass line as necessary. The basso continuo may include a harpsichord, organ, bassoon, trombone, cello, double bass, and lute or guitar.

Counterpoint was an important Baroque style commonly used by Bach, Handel, and other excellent composers of the period. Counterpoint is two independent melodies moving against each other. One is usually the soprano line, and the other is usually the bass line.

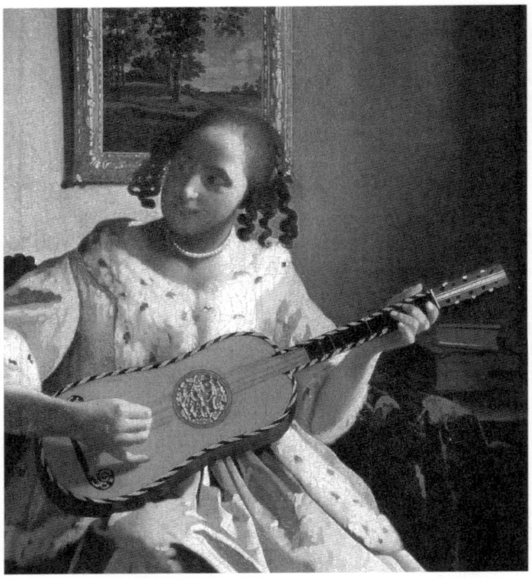

Artist Vermeer painted Baroque musician

Activity~

MUSIC

1. Look up the story of Orpheo (alias Orpheus) in mythology. Make an illustration or comic strip of the story of Orpheus.

2. Compare and contrast the opera and the oratorio. Make a chart examining their similarities and differences. You may want to extend your research to other sources.

Opera	Oratorio

3. What event of importance to America happened in 1607, the same year Monteverdi's *Orfeo* was first performed?

4. A fugue is similar to a round or canon. Try singing a round such as "Row, Row, Row Your Boat" or "White Coral Bells" with a friend.

MUSIC

George Frederick Handel, Baroque Composer

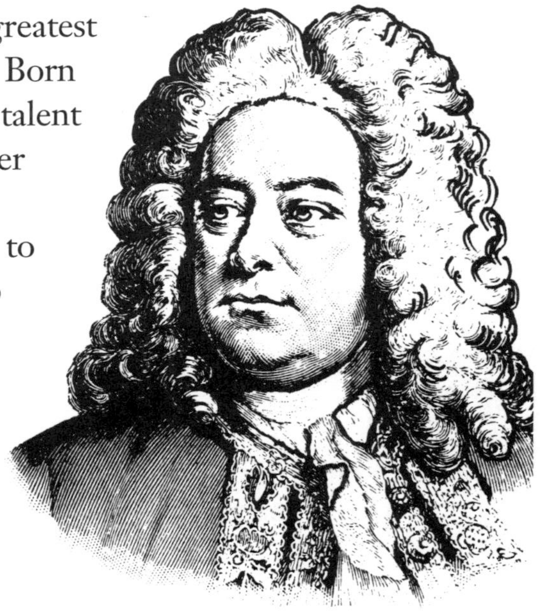

George Frederick Handel was one of the greatest composers of music in the Baroque period. Born in Halle, Germany, in 1685, he displayed a talent for music at an early age. His father, a barber and a surgeon (an interesting career combination!), did not want young George to waste his time on music. He wanted him to do something useful, such as becoming a lawyer. However, his mother managed to sneak a very quiet keyboard instrument, a clavichord, into their attic so George could practice while his father slept. Handel quickly became adept at playing keyboard instruments. His father finally agreed to allow him to take lessons. Handel spent most of his adult life in England employed as a royal court musician of King George I and later by King George's son, King George II.

Handel's music was composed in the dramatic style of the Baroque period. One of his early operas, *Rinaldo*, used recorders to imitate the sound of birds, and live sparrows were released on stage during the performance. His *Water Music*, written for orchestra, was performed for the king as he floated down the River Thames on a barge. The king's barge contained his guests, and a separate barge floated next to it which held the orchestra. *The Royal Fireworks Music*, written for orchestra to celebrate the Treaty of Aachen (Aix-la-Chapelle) in 1749, was an outdoor concert by the St. James River with a tremendous fireworks display. However, the fireworks went off too early and the launching platform caught fire, producing an explosion. When the dust cleared, two were dead and many were injured. The celebration was ruined, but the music is still wonderful.

Toward the end of the Baroque period, audiences were growing tired of the excesses displayed in operas, and the oratorio became the new style of music. The oratorio used serious religious subject matter and was performed in a church or on a stage with little or no costumes or scenery. One of the most lasting and famous of these oratorios that is still frequently performed is Handel's *Messiah*. During the first performance of this piece, the king established a tradition that is still followed today. During the part of the music known as the "Hallelujah Chorus," the king was so moved by the beauty of the music that he stood up throughout the whole section. Now in those days, when the king sat, everyone sat, and when the king stood, everyone stood. So the whole audience stood up also. Today when the "Hallelujah Chorus" is performed audiences still stand.

Activity~

1. Obtain a recording of the *Royal Fireworks Music* by George Frederick Handel from the library, a music teacher, or some other source. Listen to the first movement, called the Overture. How does Handel make this music sound like a fireworks display? How does Handel make this music sound royal?

____

____

2. The *Royal Fireworks Music* was written in five movements. A movement is a division of a larger work that may be played without the other movements, as well as a piece by itself.

- Which of the five movements (Overture, Bourree, Siciliano: "La Paix", La Rejouissance, or Menuet I-II) sounds the most like a processional for a king?

____

- Which of the five movements sounds like 18th century dance music?

____

- Which of the five movements sounds like a peaceful country scene?

____

3. Baroque music uses many decorations called ornaments. One of these ornaments is called the "trill" — a rapid moving back and forth between two notes. Select a movement to listen to. Count how many trills you can hear as you listen to it.

4. List six words that describe the music. Write a paragraph describing how this music fits into the Baroque style.

5. Draw a picture to illustrate the royal ceremony and fireworks display.

MUSIC

6. Research King George II. Write a paragraph describing him.

7. Why was the Treaty of Aachen at Aix-la-Chapelle signed?

MUSIC

Johann Sebastian Bach, Baroque Composer

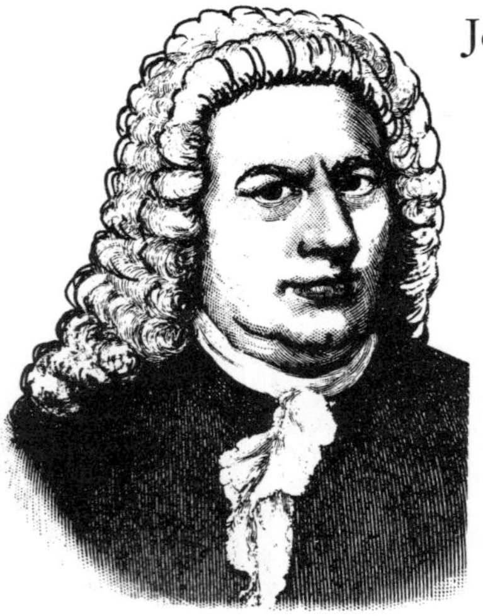

Johann Sebastian Bach

Johann Sebastian Bach was born in 1685, in what is now eastern Germany. The Bach family was famous in the area for musical ability. Young Johann Sebastian was a bright little boy who did very well in school. Johann Sebastian, orphaned at age 10, was sent to live with his older brother, Johann Christoph, an organist in Ohrdruf. (Both of his brothers were also named Johann.) Johann Sebastian was then sent to the choir school for poor boys with good singing voices. It was here that he learned to play violin, viola, and organ. Johann Sebastian Bach lived and worked in Germany all of his life.

Bach composed in all Baroque styles except opera. He was able to combine all the best qualities of the Baroque period with taste and grace. He was a master of counterpoint and the fugue. His *Toccata and Fugue in d minor* contrasts a dramatic and rhythmically free style of the toccata with the regimented form of the fugue.

MUSIC

Bach was a musical genius who was very humble about his abilities. Though he was a renowned organist, he was quoted as saying, "There is nothing to it. You have only to hit the right notes at the right time and the instrument plays itself." He never made much profit from his musical genius.

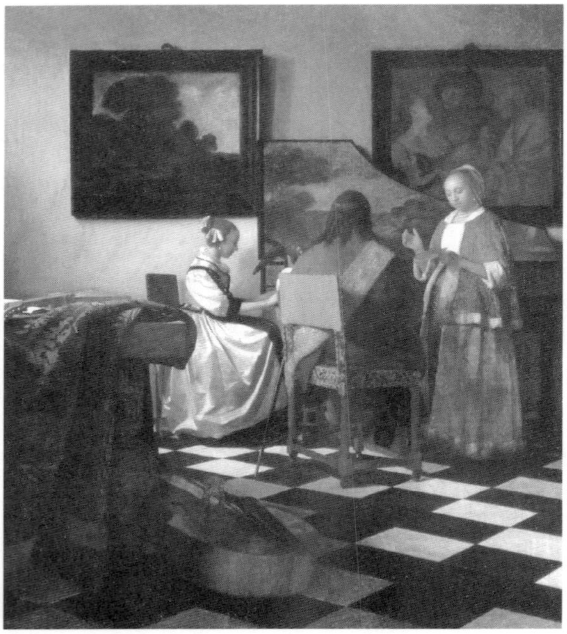

Vermeer's Baroque Musicians

Bach contributed to the popularity of the tempered (well-tuned) scale which divides the octave into 12 equal tones. This allows modulating (changing) to new keys easily without having to retune a keyboard instrument. His *The Well-Tempered Clavier*, a collection of preludes and fugues in all 12 keys, cleverly demonstrates the advantages of this system.

Bach spent much of his time as a church musician and composer of church music. He wrote over 300 sacred **cantatas** — works for soloists, chorus, and orchestra which could be considered musical sermons. Bach married twice and had 20 children, only 10 of whom lived to become adults. His wives were both musicians, as were several of his children.

Little of Bach's music was published in his lifetime and much of it was lost. More than 50 years after his death, the composer Mendelssohn discovered Bach's music again and brought it back into the public eye.

Activity~

1. Find a CD, tape, or record of the organ piece *Toccata and Fugue in d minor* by J.S. Bach from your own or a friend's collection, a library, or a music teacher. Listen to the recording. Make a list of how this music demonstrates the characteristics of the Baroque period.

   ____

   ____

   ____

2. Describe the *Toccata and Fugue in d minor* in many, varied, and unusual words. Use these words to write a haiku or draw a picture that demonstrates the words and impressions of the music.

   ____

   ____

   ____

3. More excellent Bach to try: *Brandenburg Concertos*, *The Goldberg Variations for Harpsichord*, *Suite for Orchestra*, *The Saint Matthew Passion*, and *Jesu, Joy of Man's Desiring*.

Leonardo and Harvey: Study of Anatomy and the Heart

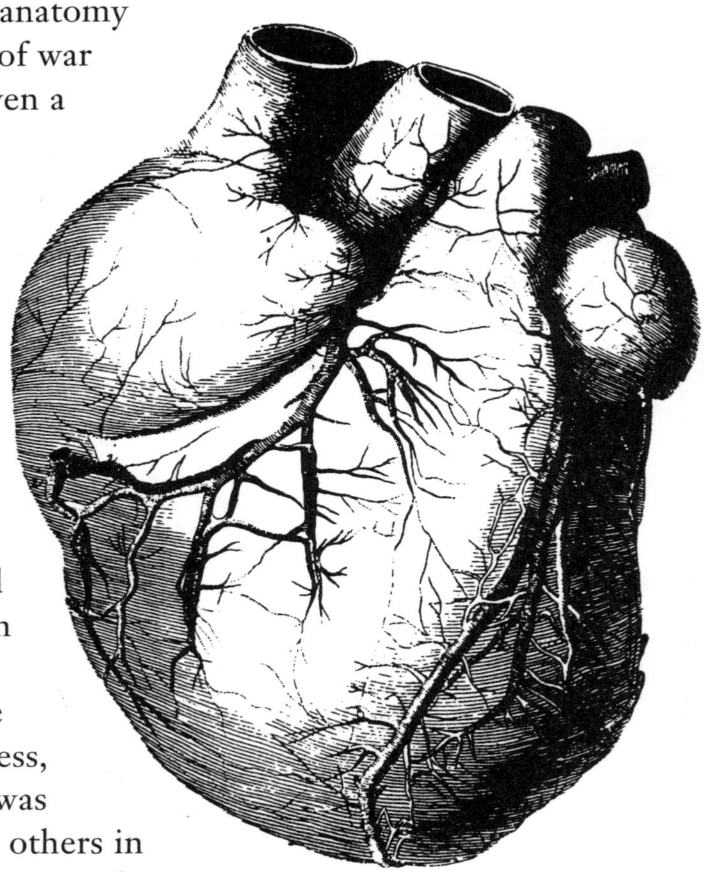

During the Renaissance there was a great deal of interest and discovery in anatomy and surgery. Often because of war wounds, physicians were given a chance to try new surgical techniques. The Renaissance was a time when there was renewed interest in human beings. Because of this interest, dissection of corpses (human beings who had died) became more common. Leonardo da Vinci, Andreas Vesalius, and others dissected bodies, then drew and wrote about their observations. Because of the invention of the printing press, this important information was passed on to others, even to others in different countries. One person in the Baroque era who read about the findings of da Vinci and Vesalius was a British doctor named William Harvey. He discovered the circulation of blood through the heart and circulatory system.

Use the diagram of the heart on the next page to study the heart and the circulatory system. Oxygen-poor blood from the body comes to the right side of the heart from the vena cavae. Blood traveling from the right atrium to the right ventricle goes to the lungs. Blood traveling from the left atrium to the left ventricle moves on to the body. Arteries carry oxygen-rich blood to cells. Veins carry oxygen-poor blood to the heart. Capillaries are the smallest blood vessels. They are the network for exchange of nutrients, waste, oxygen, and carbon dioxide. Capillaries are so small that cells need to line up to get through. Look under your tongue. The blue lines are veins, the pink ones are arteries, and the very thin lines are capillaries.

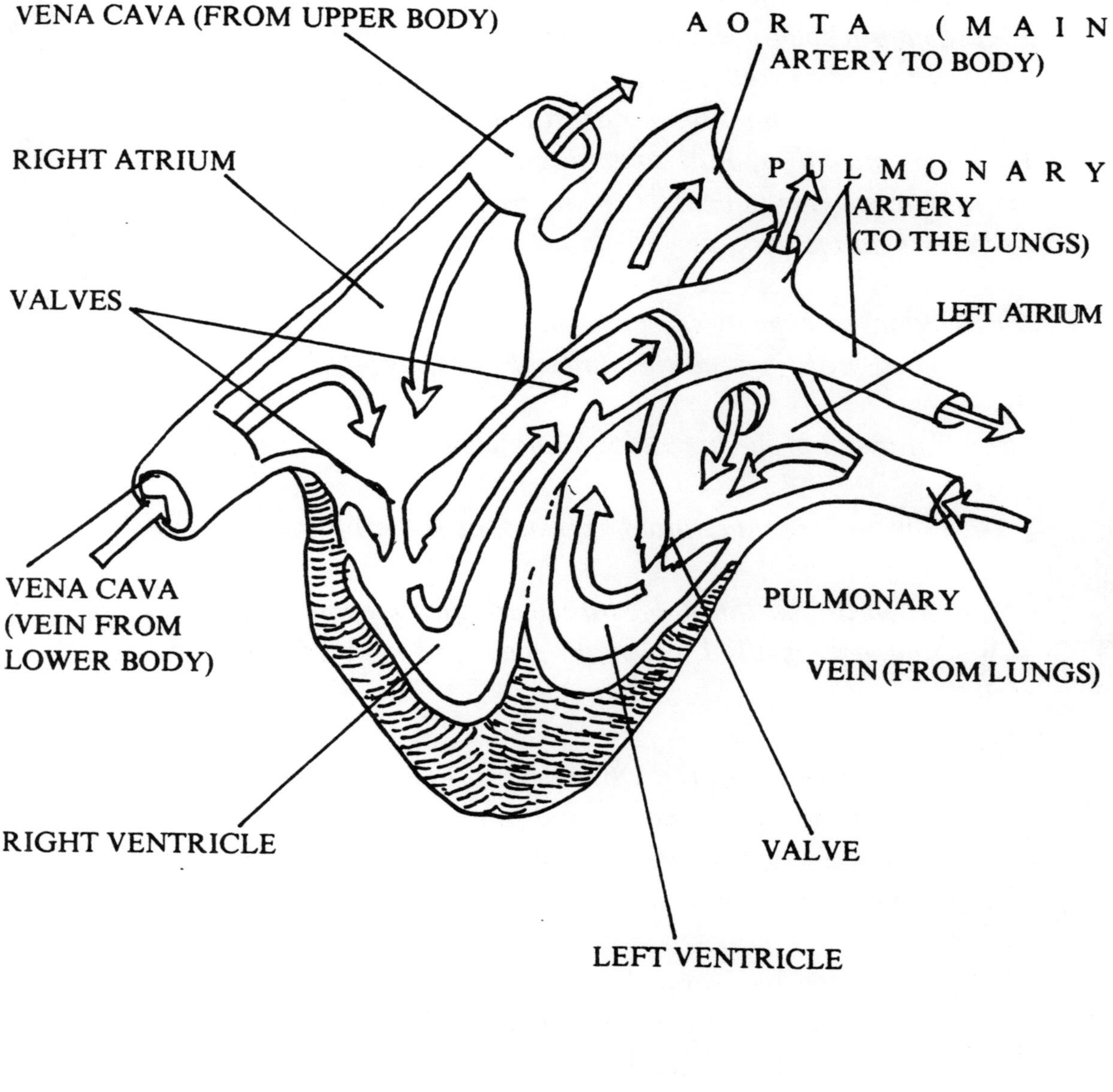

SCIENCE

Galileo

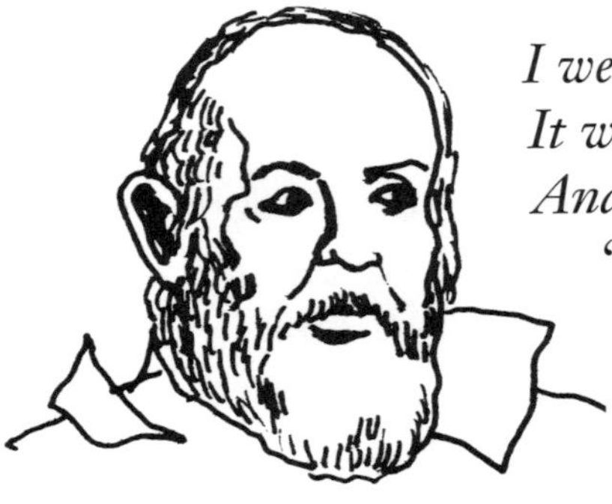

Galieleo Galilei

I went for a walk with Galileo Galilei
It was a pretty, bright, and glorious summer day
And as we walked we talked
"Mr. Galilei, tell me of your life," I said.

"Call me Galileo," and he patted me on the head.
He told me of his birth in 1564 in Pisa, Italy
and of his love for science, math, and of astronomy.

He said, "When I was your age, when I was just a boy,
I loved to play, and dream, and built a lot of my own toys.
And though it's not well known, I enjoyed my music too —
I played the organ well, and I also played the flute.
My father was a smart man, talented in every way.
He bought me all my instruments and taught me how to play.
He taught me how to paint, to be interested in all things,
he never held me back, he gave to me my wings.

'Be a doctor,' he expounded, 'but above all, be a scholar.'
So I studied medicine and the philosophy of Aristotle."

"But Galileo," I broke in, "did you not want to play and run?"

SCIENCE

"Why no," he said quite puzzled, "the learning was such fun."

Then we continued down the path, just me and Galileo,
and as we walked, I thought about this man I'd come to know.

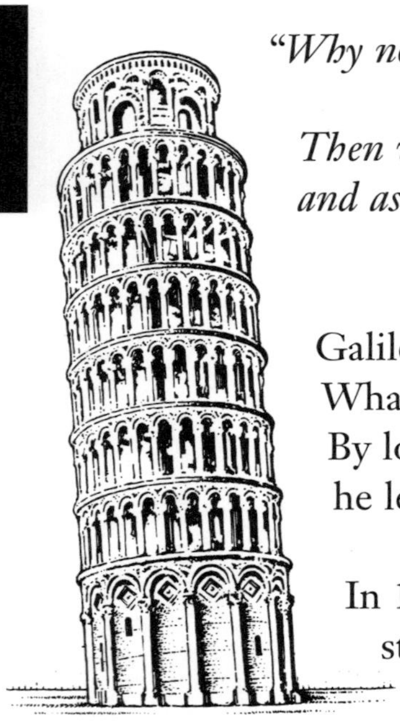

Galileo went to the University of Pisa for his college.
What he did at a young age showed his advanced knowledge.
By looking at a swinging lamp, did his first discovery come,
he learned about the human pulse and of the pendulum.

In 1585 he dropped out of school for reasons economic,
stopped his study of medicine, began again with mathematics.
At the age of twenty-five, returned to school as a professor.

Tower of Pisa

Proved the law of falling bodies; that heavier wasn't faster.

Unfortunately, his discoveries opposed those of Aristotle
which left his superiors decidedly hostile.
He quit his job at Pisa and went to work at Padua University,
Thus beginning to make his way into our works of history.

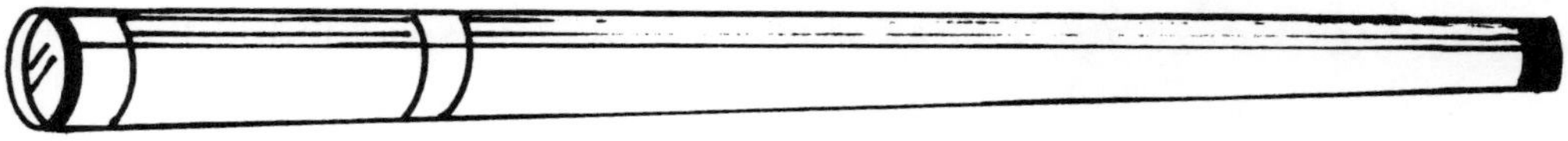

He built telescopes more powerful than had been built before,
He sold them throughout Europe and watched his fortunes soar
He gazed upon the Milky Way, he made his observations,
Ignored the literature of the day, which was fable and superstition.

In 1610 Galileo made his most famous discovery —
the four bright moons of Jupiter, which he named for the Medici.
These ideas and discoveries, brought him glory, brought him fame.
Throughout all of Europe, everyone knew his name.

But the fame, along with good, also brought the bad.
Galileo and his unique ideas had made some people mad.
For during these days in Europe, there were two schools of thought,
some people believed one way, the other people not.

The church and most Europeans, believed in theories ancient,
Galileo and more thoughtful folk had had a different education.
They believed in the theory called Copernican, named after Copernicus,
That the planets revolved around the sun, and not the likes of us!

The church tried very hard to change the thinkers of Copernican,
And when they failed, it went down hard, and all their books did ban.

"There my friend, did I get it right, the story of your life?"

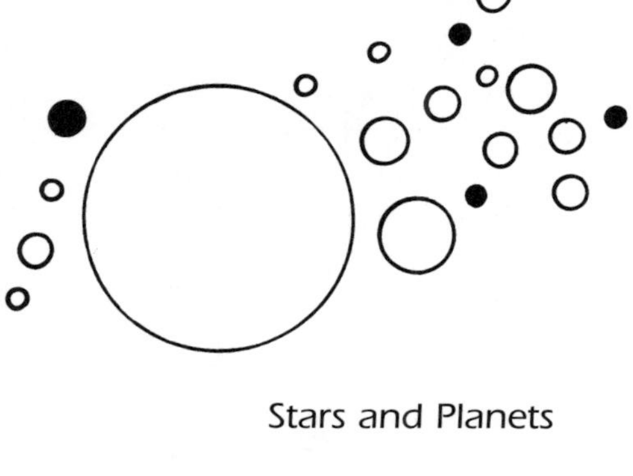

Stars and Planets

"Yes you did my son, and that's why my hair's so white.
But here's part of my story that I believe that you've omitted,
About a crime against me that was cruelly committed.

In 1632 I was brought to trial, and they finally made me say
That Copernicus was wrong and Aristotle knew the way.
But you and I know in our hearts what's wrong and what is right,
However, it took over fifty years for most people to see the light.

By then I was long gone; I didn't live to see it.
But to me, it wasn't necessary, for I always did believe it."

"I'm proud of you," I said. "You're a very important man."

"Not important, just a scholar," and then he took my hand.

We walked along together, Galileo and me,
Up to where the sun and earth and sky do meet the sea.

Activity~

Write a paragraph about Galileo and his discoveries.

____

____

____

____

____

____

____

____

____

____

COUPLETS

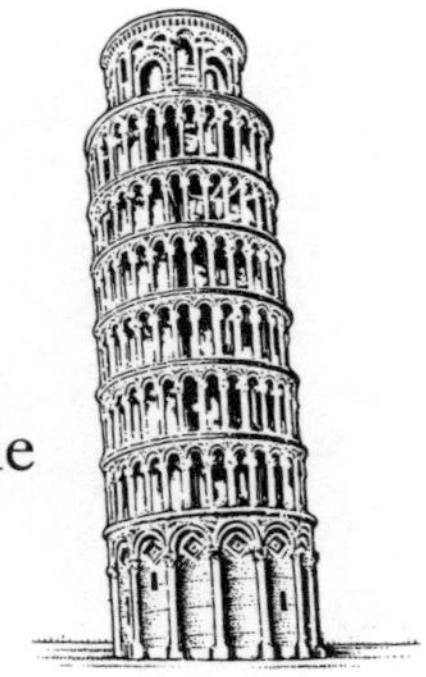

Pisa

Couplets are two lines together in a poem that rhyme. The poem about Galileo is written primarily in couplets. Answer the questions below about the life of Galileo. You will notice that each answer completes a couplet!

The stork brought Galileo to his parent's door in Pisa, Italy in __________.

Galileo enjoyed good music; he especially liked the flute. He played the organ, danced and sang, and also played the ____________________.

To the University of Pisa did Galileo come, this was where he learned about the swinging ______________________________.

The law of falling bodies does implicitly state and say that all will fall the same, no matter what its ______________________________!

The law of falling bodies makes science come alive, and to think, when he discovered it, he was only ______________________________!

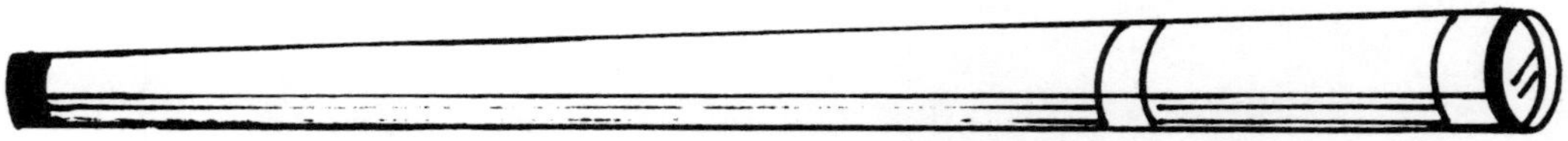

"For sale! For sale! A telescope!" We heard the vendors cry, Galileo built some mighty ones to look up in the ____________________.

The four bright moons of Jupiter Galileo he did name, his genius and discoveries brought him wealth and ____________________.

SCIENCE

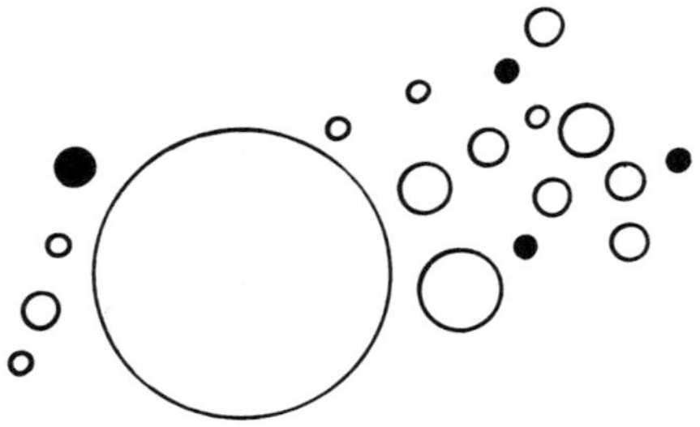

Stars and Planets

"Aristotle is quite wrong!" Galileo said, it made some people mad enough to hit him on his ______________________!

Some people didn't like him; I think it's safe to say Galileo's thinking just didn't run their ______________________.

Most scholars thought that Earth was really number one that planets revolved around the Earth and not around the ______________________.

The theory that the Earth and planets revolve around the sun is one we know is true today — it's called ______________________.

Galileo was stubborn: he wanted to have his say, for this he was punished, and in his house, he was locked ______________________.

SCIENCE

BAROQUE

WORD BOX

away	sun	way
head	lute	sky
fame	1564	pendulum
weight	25	Copernican

MAKE A THERMOMETER

In 1596 Galileo invented the thermometer. You can make a simple thermometer using a liquid, a straw, clay and a Crystal Light (Kraft Foods) container.

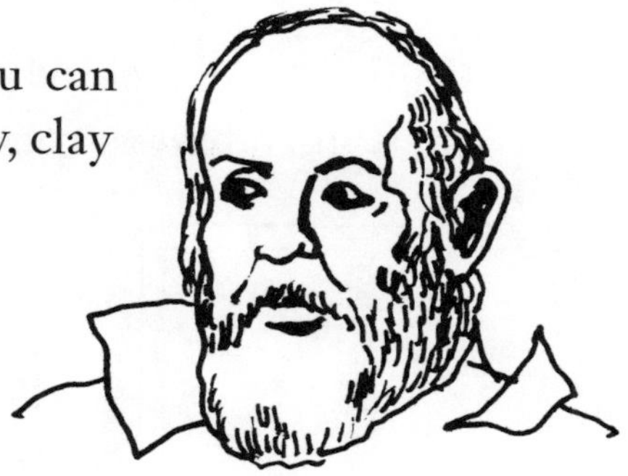

Galileo Galilei

PROCEDURE

1. Make a hole the diameter of your straw in the lid of the container.

2. Place a straw through the hole in the lid. Put clay around the straw to make a tight seal.

3. Place a liquid (water colored with food coloring or a cola) in the container so it is almost full. Put the lid on the container and continue to fill the container with liquid through the straw until the container is full and about one inch of liquid is in the straw. The straw should reach into the liquid in the container.

4. Put your thermometer in a bowl of warm water and cool water to see what happens to the level of liquid in the straw. As the liquid gets warmer, the liquid will rise in the straw. As it gets cooler, the liquid will fall. Why?

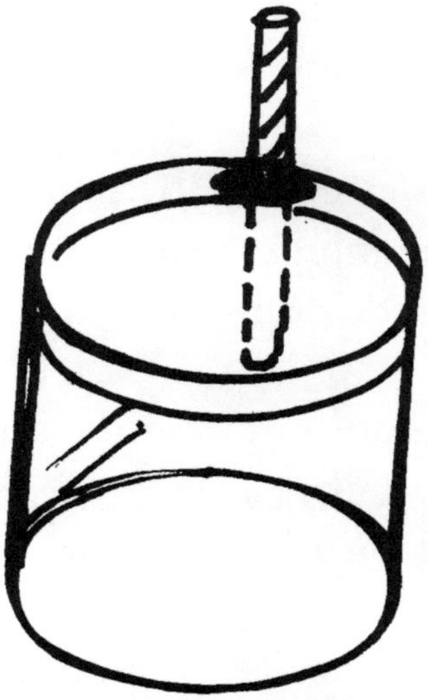

Thermometer

PENDULUM EXPERIMENT

Galileo Galilei (1564-1642) was an incredible scientist. He worked in several areas including astronomy where he studied Jupiter and the moons of Jupiter, and physics where he worked with the concept of gravity and the laws of a pendulum. His study of the pendulum with its balance and regularity reflected the ideals of the Renaissance focused on the study of nature and the simplicity and balance found in nature.

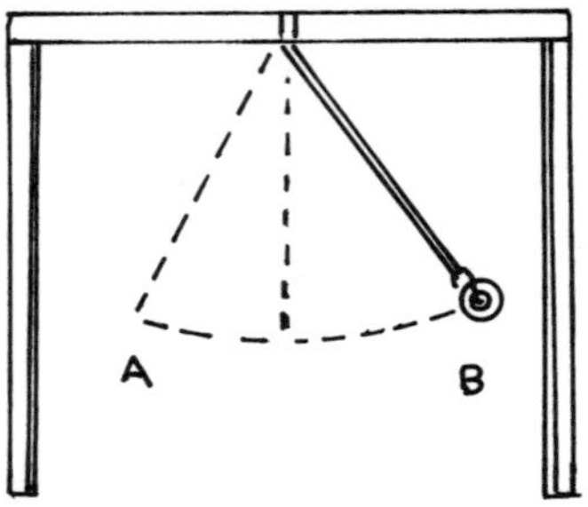

Pendulum

Try this pendulum experiment. Perhaps you could imagine your pendulum will be part of a clock, like Galileo's.

MATERIALS FOR A PENDULUM:

a string 50 cm long
a heavy washer
a paper clip separated into a backward 's' shape
tape

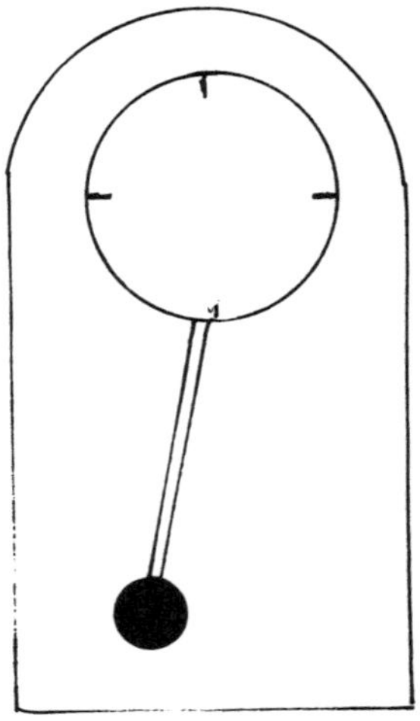
Pendulum

PROCEDURE:

1. Tie the string to the paper clip. Tape the string to the tabletop and side. Hang the washer on the clip. Measure 10 cm out from the pendulum (sideways). Mark this spot! You will start each timing from this point.

2. Set the pendulum in motion by pulling the washer to the 10 cm mark and let go. As the pendulum swings from the mark and back to it, it moves through one "period." Observe. Next, do the following experiments:

   Set the pendulum in motion. Count 30 periods and time this. Record your findings. Time____________________.
   Add a 2nd washer. Time 30 periods again, and record. Time________________.
   Add a 3rd washer. Time 30 periods again, and record. Time________________.
   What did you observe and discover?

SCIENCE

INDUCTIVE REASONING

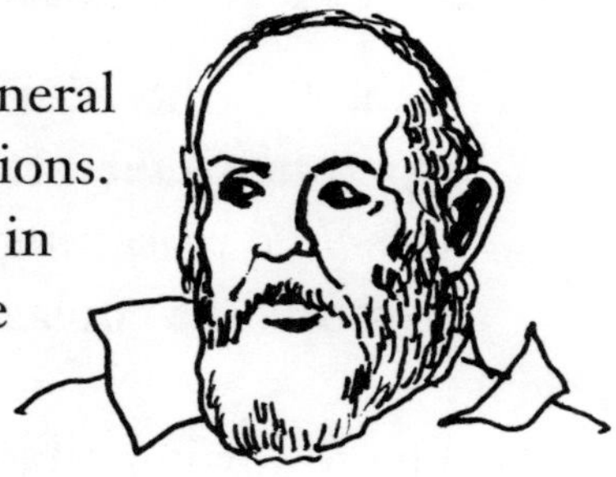

Galileo

Inductive reasoning is a method of drawing general conclusions based on a limited number of observations. Although inductive reasoning played a great part in developing mathematical ideas during the Renaissance—Baroque period, it did not prove that the ideas were correct. Two famous scientists used inductive reasoning to make important discoveries during this time period. Their discoveries were later proven true.

The Italian scientist Galileo used inductive reasoning to make several discoveries about swinging weights. His discoveries led Christian Huygens to later invent the pendulum clock.

One of Galileo's discoveries involved the length of the pendulum versus the time of its swing. His observations can be summarized in a table listing swing times for several pendulums having different lengths.

Pendulum Length	**Time of swing**
1 unit	1 second
4 units	2 seconds
9 units	3 seconds
16 units	4 seconds

1. How does the length of the pendulum seem to be related to the time of the swing? ______________________________

2. What do you think the length of a pendulum with a swing time of 5 seconds would be? ______________________________

3. What do you think the length of a pendulum with a swing time of 8 seconds would be? ______________________________

4. What do you think the length of a pendulum with a swing time of 10 seconds would be? ______________________________

answers: 1. length is square of time; 2. 25 units; 3. 64 units; 4. 100 units

INDUCTIVE REASONING 2

In 1661, the English chemist Robert Boyle did several experiments involving air pressure. His experiments used inductive reasoning to compare the volume of a gas with its pressure at a constant temperature.

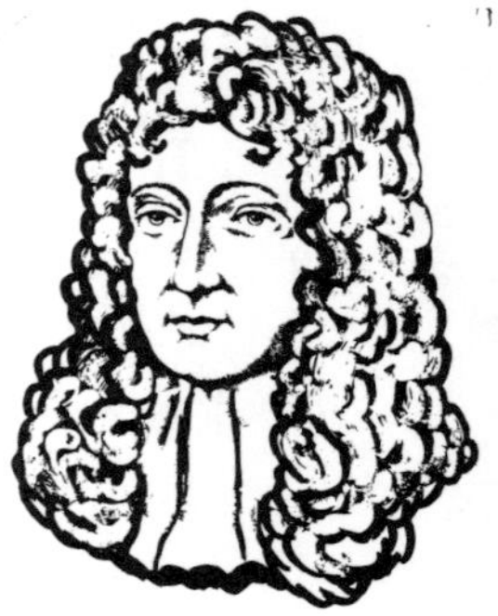

Robert Boyle

The following table lists several volumes and pressures for a gas at a constant temperature.

Boyle's Law

PV = CONSTANT

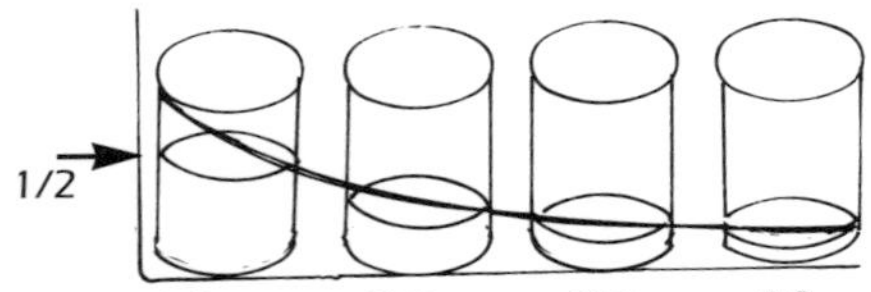

Volume	Pressure
1 unit	120 units
2 units	60 units
3 units	40 units
4 units	30 units

Activity~

From the pattern given in the table above, would it be correct to say that, when the volume is double,

1. The pressure decreases 60 units? ______________________________

2. The pressure becomes one-half of what it was? ______________________________

3. If the volume is tripled, what happens to the pressure? ______________________________

4. If the volume is multiplied by four, what happens to the pressure? ______________________________

5. When the volume is 5 units, what is the pressure? ______________________________

6. When the volume is 10 units, what is the pressure? ______________________________

answers: 1. no; 2. no; 3. it decreases by one-third; 4. it decreases by one-fourth; 5. 24 units; 6. 12 units

SCIENCE

INDUCTIVE REASONING 3

Albrecht Dürer, a famous Renaissance artist from Germany, had an interesting square of numbers in one of his paintings titled *Melancholy*. Here is the same number square with two numbers left out.

16	3	2	13
5	10	11	8
9	6	7	
4		14	1

1. What numbers do you think should go in the blanks?

____

____

2. If you assume there is a pattern in the arrangement of the numbers in the square, what kind of reasoning are you using?

____

____

3. Make up a number puzzle of your own with at least two blanks for a friend to solve.

____

____

SCIENCE

answers: 1. row 3-12, row 4-14; 2. inductive reasoning

SCIENCE AND SCIENCE FICTION

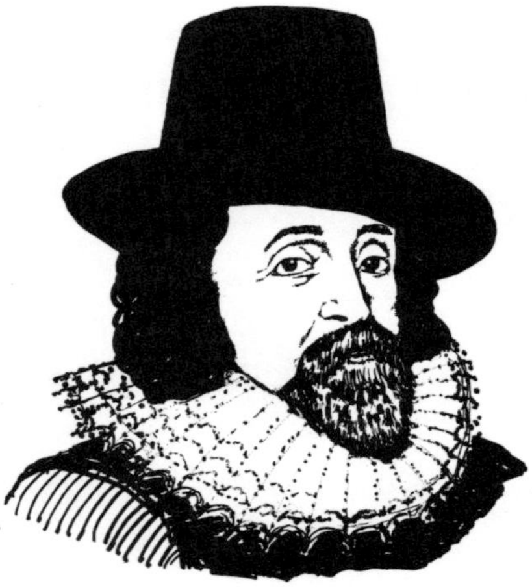

Sir Francis Bacon

Sir Francis Bacon (1561-1626) insisted that progress made in science would be based on the scientific method. The scientific method means that knowledge in science comes from experiments and discoveries rather than opinions and guesses. Bacon wrote several books including *Novum Organum*, which stated that experimentation and inductive thinking were the foundation of the scientific method. In 1626 he died after completing an experiment to test the effect of snow (cold temperature) on the rate of decay of a dead chicken.

After Sir Francis Bacon died, his science fiction book *The New Atlantis* was published. It again promoted experimentation. This book predicted robots, telephones, tape recorders, and the electric motor!

QUESTIONS:

1. What do you think the effect of cold temperature was on the rate of decay of that dead chicken in 1626? ______________________________

____

2. What is the "scientific method?" ______________________________

____

3. How long did Sir Francis Bacon live? ______________________________

____

4. List three things he predicted for the future. ______________________________

____

____

SCIENCE

BAROQUE SCIENCE FICTION

Science fiction is a form of fiction which uses scientific knowledge in a very fanciful way, often including ideas not possible at the time and which sometimes accurately predict the future.

In 1650 Cyrano de Bergerac wrote a science fiction story about traveling to the moon from earth. He discussed seven ways to get to the moon. As it turns out, the first six would not be possible, but the seventh method was the use of rockets! About 320 years after de Bergerac's story, men finally did reach the moon. How did they get there?

Write and illustrate your own science fiction story. Remember, it must be based on some scientific knowledge that can be used in your story in a fanciful way.

PASCAL'S TRIANGLE

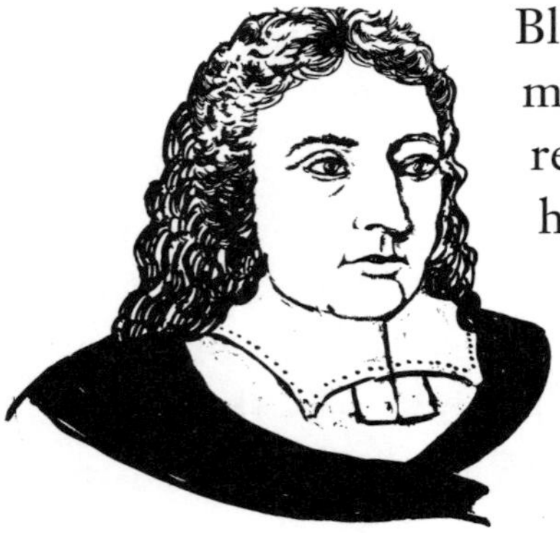

Blaise Pascal

Blaise Pascal lived from 1623 to 1662. He was a French mathematician and scientist and is remembered for his religious and philosophical writings. During his short lifetime, he invented the first mechanical adding machine and helped formulate the modern theory of probability.

The famous triangle bearing Pascal's name dates back to ancient China. It was named after Pascal because he was so interested in it and discovered many, many patterns relating to all branches of mathematics.

Here is part of Pascal's Triangle. See how many patterns you can discover. Fill in as many of the rows as you can. Notice that only eight rows are shown here, but Pascal's Triangle continues infinitely.

1 — **Row 0**
1 1 — **Row 1**
1 2 1 — **Row 2**
1 3 3 1 — **Row 3**
1 4 6 __ 1 — **Row 4**
__ __ __ __ __ __ — **Row 5**
__ __ __ __ __ __ **1** — **Row 6**
__ __ __ __ __ __ __ __
__ __ __ __ __ __ __ __ __

1. Sum the numbers in each of the first several rows of Pascal's Triangle. The first three are done for you.

Row	0	1	2	3	4	5	6
Sum	1	2	3				

2. What is the pattern of the sum?

____

3. How could you relate the sum of the row to the row number?

4. How could you express the sum of the elements of the 25th row?

5. What is the sum of the 100th row?

6. What patterns do you see in these diagonals?
   - a) 1, 2, 3, 4, 5, _, _, _, _, _These are the counting numbers
   - b) 1, 3, 6, 10, _, _, _, _, _ These are triangular numbers.

7. Do you see any other patterns?

For other ideas see *Visual Patterns in Pascal's Triangle* by Dale Seymour Publications.

answers: 1. 8, 16, 32, 64; 2. they are powers of 2; 3. sum is 2n where n is the row number; 4. 225; 5. 2100

BAROQUE COMPUTER HISTORY HEXAGRAM

During the seventeenth century, many inventions were made involving mechanical calculators. Mathematicians such as Blaise Pascal developed the Pascaline to help his father with his job. John Napier invented a set of rods to help multiply by only adding. Samuel Moreland developed a calculator that could add and subtract to help compute taxes, and Gottfried von Leibniz developed a calculator called the Stepped Reckoner that could do all four operations. These inventions were a technological breakthrough and the rudimentary beginnings of our computer history.

Use the clue to help learn more about these early calculator inventors. Complete each vertex of the hexagon by unscrambling the letters. The following clues may help you. Every vertex point must also use the letter contained in the center of the hexagon.

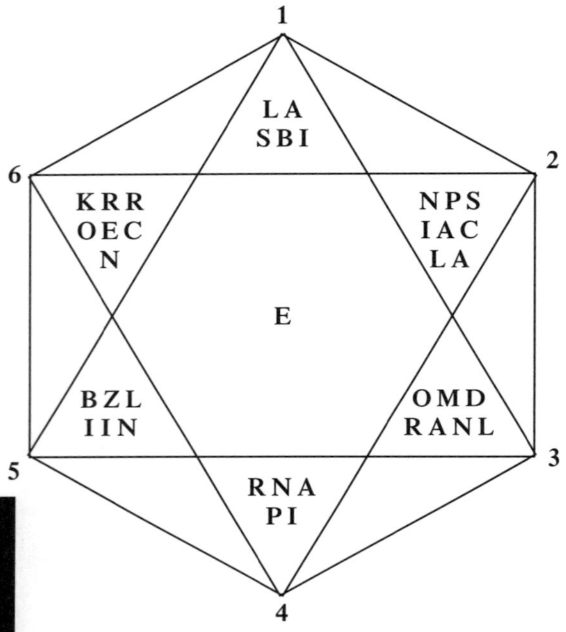

HEXAGON CLUES

1. He invented the first mechanical adding machine while he was still a teenager. _______________ Pascal

2. This adding machine was called the _________________________________.

3. He computed the taxes for France with a calculator he built that could add and subtract. ___________________________

4. He invented a set of rods made of "bones" to make multiplication and division easier. ____

5. He invented the first calculator that could successfully add, subtract, multiply, and divide. ____

6. This calculator was called the Stepped _______________________________.

MAKE YOUR OWN HEXAGRAM

Use any subject you wish appropriate to the Renaissance-Baroque time period (1500-1700 AD).

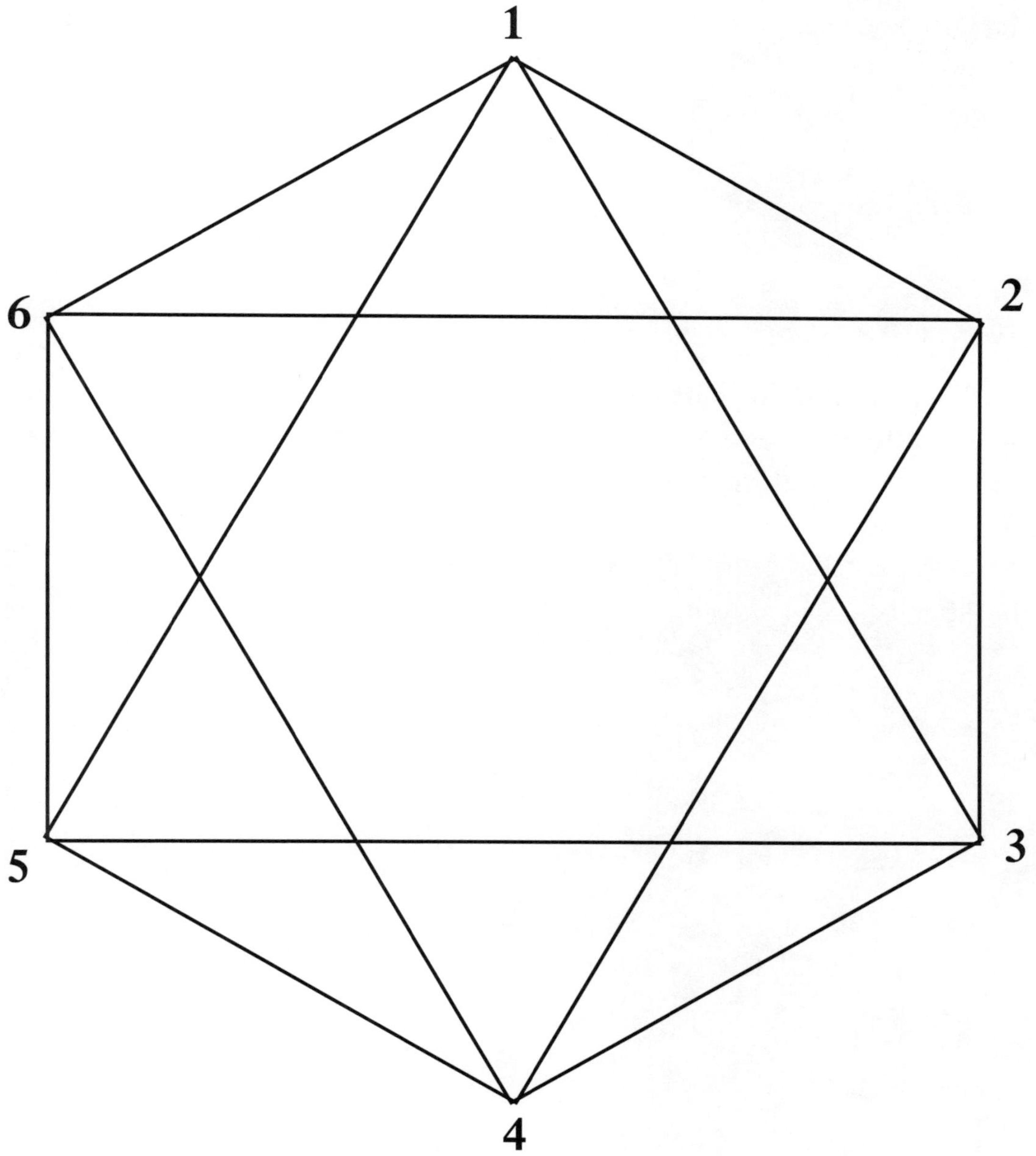

SCIENCE

THE RENAISSANCE AND BAROQUE FOOD CHAIN

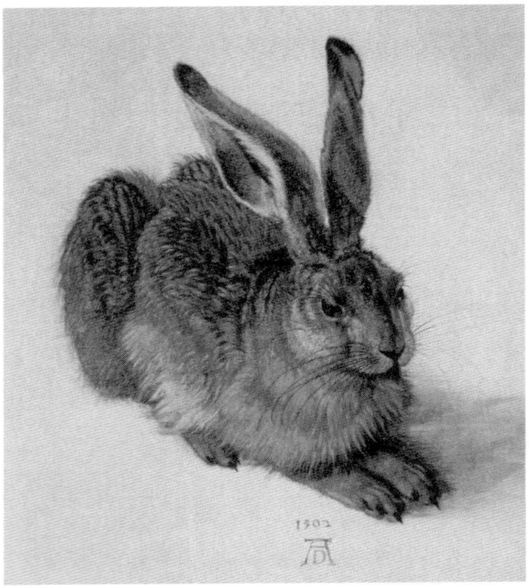

Dürer's HARE

People of the Renaissance spent much of their time studying nature. The results of this study can be seen in many paintings of the time. Renaissance artist Albrecht Dürer painted a lifelike and realistic portrait of a rabbit. During the Baroque era, when animals were painted they were sometimes portrayed with great emotion. An example of that is Peter Paul Rubens' *Daniel in the Lion's Den*.

All animals (including rabbits and lions) are a part of the food chain. Children can play a game that demonstrates the food chain. Provide each child with a card labeling them as a plant, plant-eater, or meat-eater. Each child then finds a place in the "chain" according to what they are — plants with plant-eaters, meat-eaters with plant-eaters. What happens when there are not enough spots for everyone on the "chain?"

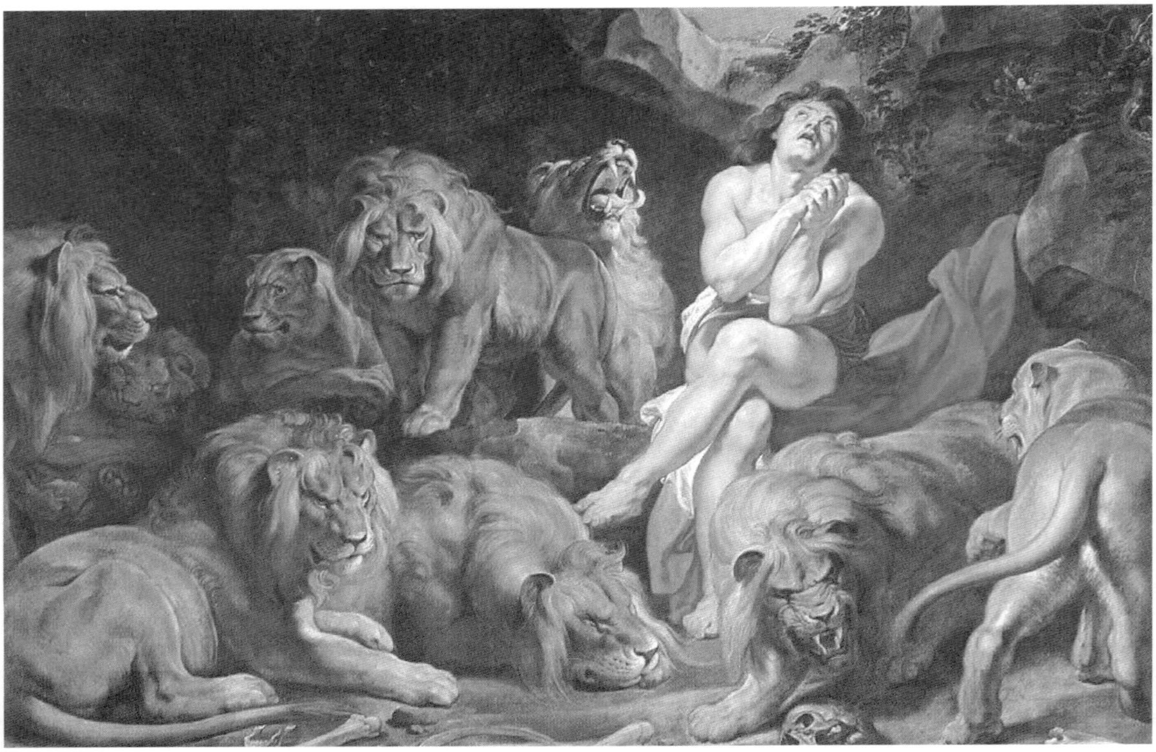

Ruben's DANIEL IN THE LION'S DEN

THINGS NEVER SAID BY BAROQUE INVENTORS

Create your own ridiculous saying for each inventor. Make it relate to what they invented.

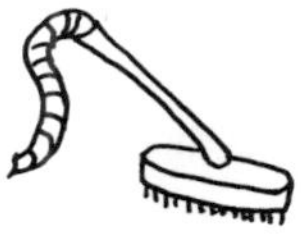

"My wife would just love to vacuum." HUYGENS

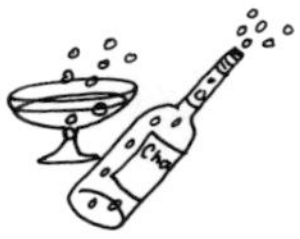

"I hope I can get the bubbles out." DOM PERIGNON

"A steam what?" THOMAS SAVERY

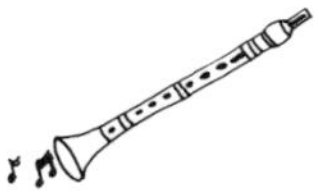

"Let me serenade you." DENNER

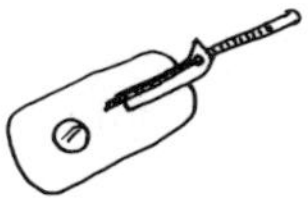

"Now I can thread a needle." LEEUWENHOEK

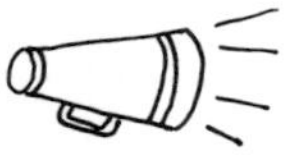

"Can you hear me now?" MORLAND

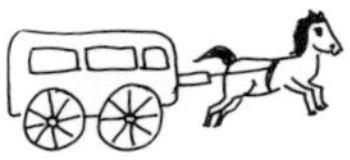

"Is this the bus to downtown?" PASCAL

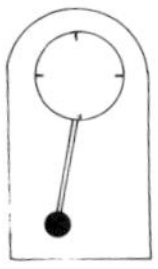

"Does it ever stop ticking?" LIPPERSHEY

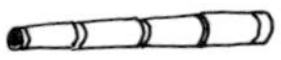

"It's not very clear." GUERICKE

SCIENCE

BAROQUE INVENTOR MATCH

_____1. Christian Huygens
_____2. Otto von Guericke
_____3. Dom Perignon
_____4. Hans Lippershey
_____5. Blaise Pascal
_____6. Sir Samuel Morland
_____7. Anton van Leeuwenhoek
_____8. Johann Christopher Denner
_____9. Thomas Savery

A. invented a steam pump
B. invented a megaphone
C. invented a precision microscope
D. invented the clarinet
E. invented champagne
F. invented the omnibus
G. invented the obscure telescope
H. invented the pendulum clock
I. invented the vacuum pump

answers: 1.i, 2.g, 3.e, 4.h, 5.f, 6.b, 7.c, 8.d, 9.a

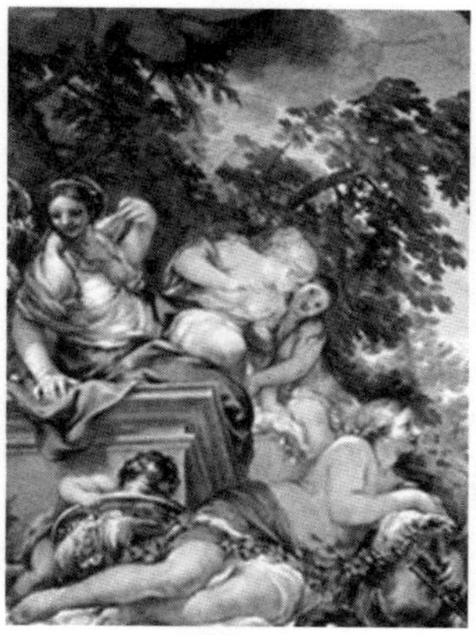

The Rococo Era

Rococo art and architecture reflected the lifestyle of the nobility in Europe following the Baroque period. Rococo was the prevailing style during the reign of Louis XV and then into other European countries such as Germany and Austria. Rococo is characterized by excessive use of gold, intricate curves, ornamentation, and relentless decoration. The architecture is like a wedding cake whose decorator went berserk.

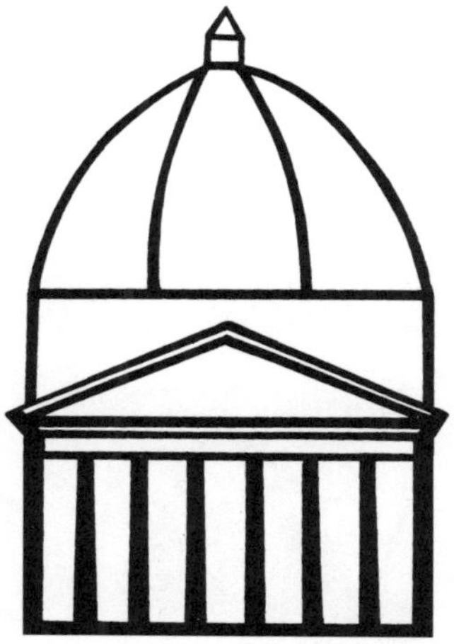

Renaissance

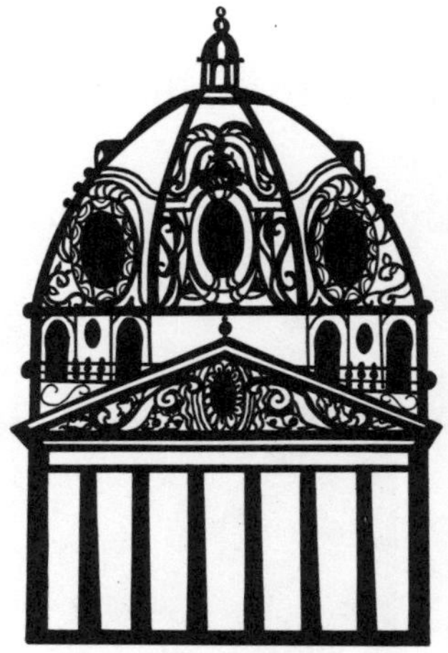

Baroque

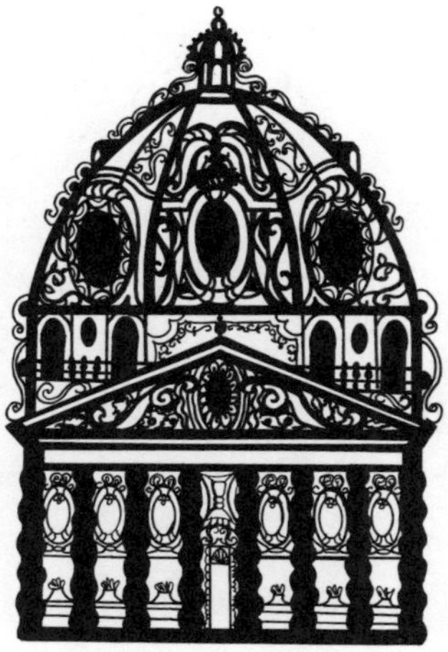

Rococo

Activity~

Make this ordinary building interior into an example of Rococo. Remember that Baroque had large sweeping curves while Rococo had smaller, more intricate curlicues.

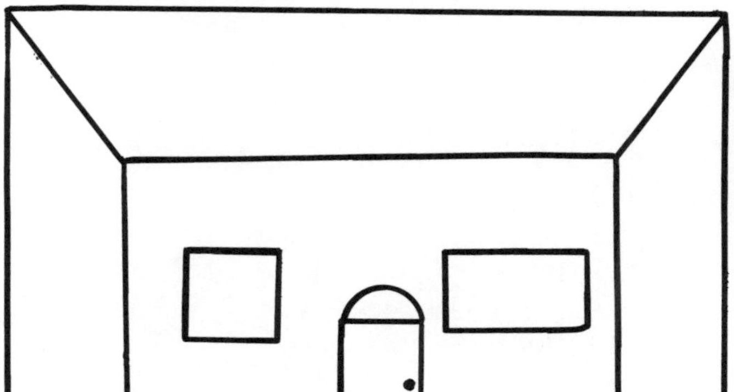

ROCOCO PAINTING

Rococo is a style associated with obsession with merriment, gaiety, pleasure, playfulness, and frivolity. Rococo artists used pretty colors on pretty people in beautiful, artificial settings often with pastel-tinted clouds.

The French artist Francois Boucher's (1703-1770) paintings show the nobility living a life devoted to frivolous pleasure. Sometimes his work would include mythology.

The Rococo occurred shortly before the French, American, and other revolutions. Do you think there is a connection between the elaborate life style of royalty and ordinary people revolting against them?

Compare the Rococo painting with that of Raphael's *St. Sebastian* from the Renaissance.

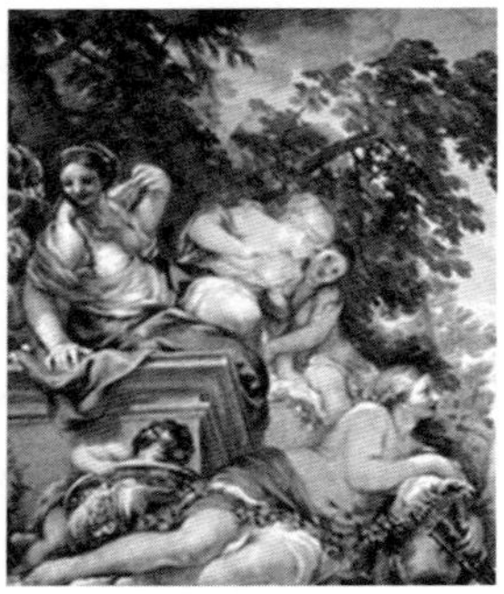

ROCOCO PAINTING

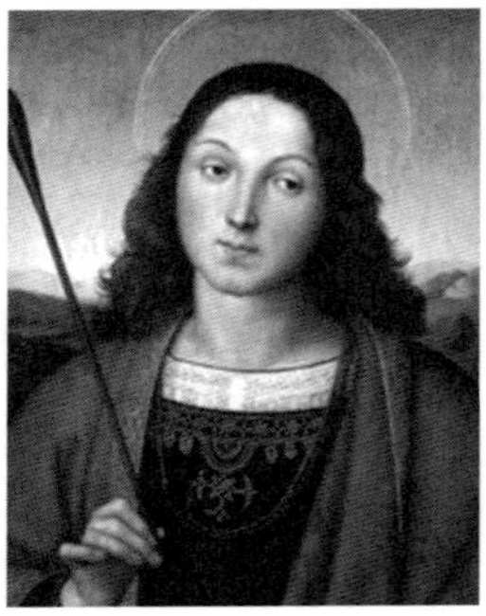

RAPHAEL

TIME PERIOD	______________	______________
LOCATION	______________	______________
CLOTHING	______________	______________
LIFE'S IDEALS	______________	______________
LIFE LIVED FOR	______________	______________
SINGLE WORDS TO DESCRIBE	______________	______________

BAROQUE AND ROCOCO EVALUATION

In this unit you have learned about artists and their artwork, inventors and their inventions as well as famous architecture built during this era. Use your productive thinking skills to choose:

1. One of my favorite inventions from this time period is the ______________

   ____.

   It was invented by ____.

   It was used to ____.

2. One of my favorite paintings from this unit was ______________________.

   The artist who did this work was ___________________________________.

   It shows ____.

3. A work of architecture I learned about was __________________________.

   It is located in ____.

   Some of its features are ____.

4. A famous person from this period is _______________________________.

   He was famous for ____.

5. If I had lived in the Baroque time I would have been a

   ____________________________ and ______________________________.

REVIEW

BAROQUE AND ROCOCO REVIEW

1.__________________proved that the heart pumps blood.

2.__________________was a famous woman artist.

3.__________________painted *Daniel and the Lion's Den.*

4.__________________painted *The Night Watch.*

5.__________________perfected the telescope and invented the thermometer.

6.__________________was the Baroque artist who used dramatic realism and *chiaroscuro.*

7.__________, ____________, and Rembrandt were famous Baroque Dutch artists.

8.__________________was the architect for St. Paul's Cathedral.

9. ____________________was the most famous Baroque palace.

10. ____________________was a famous Rococo painter.

11.__________________was a time period devoted to pleasure.

BAROQUE

WORD **BOX**

Galileo	Versailles
Harvey	Rembrandt
Boucher	Gentileschi
Rubens	Rococo
Caravaggio	Vermeer
Hals	

LETTERS HOME

You have just completed your visit to the Baroque and Rococo time period. Write a letter home describing your visit.

Date:____________________

Dear__________________________ ,

____

____

____

____

____

____

____

____

With emotion,

____

Draw an illustration for your letter.

REVIEW

Bibliography For Baroque And Rococo

Burns, Edward. *Western Civilizations*. Norton.
Canaday, John. *Mainstreams of Modern Art*. Holt, Rinehart, Winston.
Clark, Judith. *History of Art*. Mallard Press.
Clark, Kenneth. *Civilisation*. Harper & Row.
Cole, Bruce and Gealt, Adelheid. *Art of the Western World*. Summit Books.
Dorra, Henri. *Art in Perspective*. Harcourt Brace Jovanovich.
Garder, Helen. *Art Through the Ages*. Harcourt Brace.
Hartt, Frederick. *Italian Renaissance Art*. Prentice-Hall.
Hollingsworth, Patricia and Hollingsworth, Stephen. *Smart Art*. Zephyr Press.
Jacobs, Jay. *Encyclopedia of World Art*. Octopus Books.
Janson, H. W. *History of Art*. Prentice Hall.
Platt, Richard. *Smithsonian Visual Timeline of Inventions*. Dorling Kindersley.
Steves, Rick and Openshaw, Gene. *Europe 101*. John Muir Publications.
Strickland, Carol and Boswell, John. *The Annotated Mona Lisa*. Universal Press.
Turvey, Peter. *Timelines Inventions*. Franklin Watts.
Winters, Nathan. *Architecture is Elementary*. Gibbs Smith Publisher.

Music Bibliography

Apel, Willi. *Harvard Dictionary of Music*.
Barber, David. *Bach, Beethoven, and the Boys*.
Kruckenberg, Swen. *The Symphony Orchestra and its Instruments*.